5 August

D1279723

REALITY CONSTRUCTION
IN SOCIETY

REALITY CONSTRUCTION
IN SOCIETY

by

BURKART HOLZNER

University of Pittsburgh

SCHENKMAN PUBLISHING COMPANY, INC.

CAMBRIDGE, MASSACHUSETTS

301
H762r
cop. 2

LMS

Copyright © 1968

SCHENKMAN PUBLISHING COMPANY, INC.

Cambridge, Massachusetts 02138

PRINTED IN THE UNITED STATES OF AMERICA

Library of Congress Catalog Card Number: 67-29325

ALL RIGHTS RESERVED. THIS BOOK, OR PARTS THEREOF,
MAY NOT BE REPRODUCED IN ANY FORM WITHOUT
WRITTEN PERMISSION OF THE PUBLISHERS.

Contents

UNIVERSITY LIBRARIES
CARNEGIE-MELLON UNIVERSITY
PITTSBURGH, PENNSYLVANIA 15213

Preface

This book explores the systematic scope of the sociology of knowledge. It integrates phenomenological, and traditional sociological, and social psychological perspectives. Such an enterprise requires a highly general overview of a very large domain of social scientific knowledge, and the maintenance of a consistent perspective throughout. I have deliberately avoided historical discussions of the manifold divergent approaches used in the sociology of knowledge. The essay concentrates on the subject matter of society and knowledge; it is not an overview of sociological approaches or theoretical traditions.

I have tried to understand the processes of knowledge formation in the "construction" and interpretation of experienced reality, their inherent characteristics, their links to the processes structuring social systems, and their distribution and organization in societies. The organization of the materials presented, and even the language used serve to focus on the interdependencies of knowledge formation with social processes; I think that they make even familiar facts appear in a somewhat different light.

Since the manuscript was completed in the Spring of 1966 Peter Berger and Thomas Luckmann published their interesting book *The Social Construction of Reality.* * I have in no way modified my essay, thereafter, but I do feel that the two publications complement each other in many ways. One of the main differences in emphasis is my explicit concern with the structured distribution of knowledge in differentiated social systems, and the conditions of its maintenance and change. Throughout this book the concept "social system" is of central importance.

Even this modest work owes much to the help of many people. I must thank the Social Science Research Institute of the University of Hawaii, and especially its Director, Dr. William P. Lebra, for enabling me to complete this manuscript. My friends who read the essay in various stages, and who helped me with their suggestions, have my deep gratitude. Among the especially diligent readers were Dr. John K. Rhoads, Dr. Ratna Dutta, Dr. Takie Lebra, Mr. Bliss Cartwright, and Mr. Ian Stone.

Burkart Holzner

Pittsburgh, Pa.
September, 1967

Part 1
THE SOCIAL CONSTRUCTION
OF REALITY

Chapter I

The Diversity of Reality

"Self" and "World" and the Unity of Experienced Reality

Every person experiences the reality of the situations which he confronts in the course of his normal, everyday activities as directly and immediately given; he is obviously certain of his own reality and of the existence of the things he knows. Likewise, he extends this certainty of knowing the reality of existing things to many matters which he merely knows of, or about; but there are many shades and degrees of firmness and certitude involved. In the natural attitude of everyday life we do not live in doubt but in acceptance of reality. Nothing appears so strange to us as the philosophical or even the scientific doubt that things may not be what they appear to be. Few thoughts are as disquieting as the notion that the reality which we experience may be the result of social construction.

Not only is the existence of reality immediately certain in our experience, but we are also inclined to ascribe to it some general qualities. Above all, we tend to see reality as a unitary, connected world in which we live as unitary, integral selves. Alfred Schutz has described the reality of the world of daily life. He means by the term "world of daily life" the intersubjective world which precedes our own life and which has been given an interpretation by others. We are certain that we perceive it as others perceive it.

In the moment of present experience this structured world is given to our interpretation. Such interpretation is based on previous experience and the resulting "knowledge at hand." It is anchored in a general scheme of reference.

We "know" with great certainty that the world in which we live consists of determinate objects, among which we may move about, which constrain and resist us, and upon which we may act. To the non-reflective "natural attitude" of everyday life the world is inherently organized. We may, reflectively, subject our own experience to psychological and philosophical analysis in order to explain its nature. But: "The natural

1

attitude does not know these problems. To it the world is from
the outset not the private world of the single individual, but the
intersubjective world common to all of us, in which we have
not a theoretical but an eminently practical interest. The world
of everyday life is the scene and also the object of our actions
and interactions. We have to dominate it and we have to change
it in order to realize the purposes which we pursue within it
among our fellow men. We work and operate not only within
but upon the world." *

We know this natural world to be real, and we know it to
be open to exploration. It may yield us surprises, as the hitherto unexplored hidden side of an object comes into view. But
even in this kind of surprise, we are merely confirmed in our
knowledge of the reality and firmness of the world, of its independence from our own capricious wishes or whims: it displays
itself to our exploration as it is. Such surprise at discovering a
hidden valley, or a spot of ink on the surface of the desk may
be profound or trivial; in either case it illustrates to us our firm
conviction that we discover reality, we do not construct it. The
surprise of this kind is totally different from the "reality shock",
the surprising and jolting experience of being confronted by the
irreality of something previously "known" to be real, or by the
experience that others do not view our reality as we do, or by
meaningless events. In the surprise of discovery we find something that all others now might see, and that was there before
we found it; in the surprise of the reality shock we are confronted by the fragility of what in the natural attitude is the
very source of firmness and certitude itself.

Our own acts and projects relate to this real world of everyday life which they may explore or change. Action is, in fact,
dependent on the conviction of reality. When we commit ourselves to a project, to be "realized" through our acting, we know
that the outcome, to be brought about in the future, may be
uncertain. The uncertainty of action is tolerable only within a
framework of certainties, the most basic of which is the shared
actuality of real things experienced in the moment of acting,
and the certainty that I am acting.

The moment of actuality, of doing something with known

*Alfred Schutz, *Collected Papers*, Volume I, "The Problem of Social
Reality," Martinus Nijhoff, The Hague, Netherlands, 1962, p. 208. It is
clear that my analysis owes much to this work.

things here and now, confronts us with irrevocable reality. It cannot be taken back. The same holds for the experience of our own self. Merleau-Ponty illuminates this point in his discussion of a quote from Descartes who writes in his Third Meditation: "Let who will deceive me, the fact remains that he cannot cause me to be nothing when I think I am something; or cause it to be true one day that I have never existed, since it is true that I now exist." To this Merleau-Ponty adds that the experience of the present contains an assurance of existence once and for all. "In the certitude of the present there is an intention which outruns the presentness of the present, which posits it in advance of an indubitable "former present" in the series of recollections, and perception as knowledge of the present is the central phenomenon which makes possible the unity of the ego, and with it the ideas of objectivity and truth." *

The continuity of my own identity is just as implied in the experience of present, actual reality as the continuity of the world. Self and world do imply each other in our experience and there is a necessary structural correspondence between them. Our tendency to think of reality as a unified world thus corresponds to our tendency to think of ourselves as unitary, identical over time. Reality, as experienced by us in the natural attitude of everyday life, is a simple given. It is open to exploration and yields sometimes surprise discoveries, thus confirming its independence of our self and its wishes. Our actions are obviously intertwined with it, even though it is in action that we "realize" most directly the juxtaposition of world and self. Corresponding to our naive "knowledge" of the unity of the real world, there is our naive "knowledge" of the unity of our own self, and there is our faith that both these realities appear to others as they appear to us.

Multiple Realities: The Multiplicity of Reality in the Experience of the Agent

So far we have had to emphasize the naive conviction of the unity and coherence of reality. Yet, we cannot simply let matters go at that. Looking at our own experience and that of others from the point of view of the detached observer, we discover immediately that there are several types of reality, and that

*Maurice Merleau-Ponty, *Phenomenology of Perception*, translated from the French by Colin Smith, New York, The Humanities Press, 1962, p. 44.

their coherence is problematic. It is true that in the actual experience of confronted reality we tend to experience the unity and coherence of self and world which we discussed. But in reflection we see that there are many "sub-universes" of reality, as William James called them. Let us turn to the classic exposition of the issue in the work of William James, who points out that there are many categories of illusion and reality. ". . . alongside of the world of absolute error (i.e., error confined to single individuals) but still within the world of absolute reality (i.e., reality believed by the complete philosopher) there is the world of collective error, there are the worlds of abstract reality, of relative or practical reality, of ideal relations, and there is the supernatural world. The popular mind conceives of all these sub-worlds more or less disconnectedly; and when dealing with one of them, forgets for the time being its relations to the rest." *

But the philosopher, according to James, must determine the place of a given object in any one of these "sub-worlds", and he should determine "the relations of each sub-world to the others in the total world which *is.*" James' approach to the problem differs from ours in that it is not just descriptive and explanatory, but evaluative and his explanations are restricted to psychology. Still, his listing of "sub-universes" of reality holds interest.**

There is, first, the world of sensory experience, or of physical things "as we instinctively apprehend them, with such qualities as heat, color, and sound, and such 'forces' as life, chemical affinity, gravity, electricity, all existing as such within or on the surface of things." Secondly, we have the world of science, or of descriptive and explanatory constructions in the search for laws. Third, we all know the world of "ideal relations," as we find it in logic, mathematics, ethics, or other formal disciplines. Fourth, James lists the "world of 'idols of the tribe,' illusions or prejudices common to the race. All educated people recognize these as forming one sub-universe." Yet, in giving his examples, he must recognize that the "scientific truth" of one period may become the "idol of the tribe" of another. The "sub-universe" is not as unitary as it seems.

*William James, *The Principles of Psychology,* Encyclopedia Britannica Co., 1952, p. 641.
**William James, op. cit.

The many supernatural worlds are listed fifth. There are "the Christian heaven and hell, the world of the Hindu mythology, the world of Swedenborg's visa et audita, etc. Each of these is a consistent system, with definite relations among its own parts. Neptune's trident, e.g., has no status of reality whatever in the Christian heaven; but within the classic Olympus certain definite things are true of it, whether one believes in the reality of the classic mythology as a whole or not." Sixth, we find the "various worlds of individual opinion, as numerous as men are." And then there are, seventh, "the worlds of sheer madness and vagary, also indefinitely numerous." *

Any percept or object of thought becomes real for us, James asserts, if it enters into a relation to our emotional, active life. It is our concern with it, and our attention to it, which endows it with the quality of reality. As our attention and concern shift, so does the reality which we apprehend. "Each world whilst it is attended to is real after its own fashion; only the reality lapses with the attention." **

Upon inspection of our past experiences we must admit that our concern was at different times with different "sub-universes" of reality, and that the feeling of unity could be maintained for the moment only, because we did not attend to conflicting points of view. Whether we accept James' list of reality types is quite immaterial; it should be taken merely as an illustration. There may be as many "sub-universes" as there are different vital concerns of ours, and different modes of symbolic representation. From this perspective, the self and the real world appear differentiated. We must admit now to many different ways of apprehending reality, or of 'constructing' it.

Of all the domains of reality the paramount one is the reality of "things". This is what Emile Durkheim had in mind when he tried to specify the nature of the scientific method. Science, he argued, deals with facts, and facts are "things". A "thing", like the furniture we use, is external to us, and it imposes constraints which we are powerless to ignore. Things are tangible, tastable, audible; they exist for us in an integration of various sense data. Most importantly, they are manipulable. We can do something with them, and in manipulation, we can experience

*William James, The Principles of Psychology, Encyclopedia Britannica Co., 1952, pp. 641-642.

**William James, The Principles of Psychology, op. cit., p. 643.

a confirmation of what we perceive. There occurs a match between acting and knowing. The thing which we handle must fit into both conceptions and potential plans about it. It constrains us by offering resistance.

These manipulable things, directly experienced by us, have the quality of "actuality." They are, as Alfred Schutz puts it, a part of our "vivid present." This means that the perception of a thing is experientially immediate or "non-inferential." It is lived as "actual" in full consciousness. The experienced actuality is normally considered a shared one. Two persons in communication with each other share the same vivid present by including each other in their awareness.*

The thing before both of us is experienced as real by us because it is a directly given component of our vivid present. It has "actuality," and it may be directly confirmed by the experience of manipulation. The actual moment of reality experience, however, is not an isolated incident. It is placed into at least four different contexts within the person's experience. By being located in those broad and basic contexts, an actual experience is assigned some meaning. The contexts or extensions of reality experience are: first, the extension of time and space; second, the extension of symbolism and of symbolic possibilities; third, the extension of values; and fourth, the extension of communication. Certain more limited aspects of all these, that is more specific domains of placement of experience within these contexts, are called frames of reference or systems or orientation. We discuss these at a later stage.

The vivid present, containing an array of objects, soon turns into the world of the past. But since at one time it was manipulable by us, or within our reach, it turns into the world of "restorable reach" (Schutz). We can restore the manipulations of the past, at least in general, and can say: "I did it once; I can do it again." The reality of the lived moment is, of course, also extended into the future, but in a different way: the future is a projection based upon the regularities found in the world of restorable reach. Schutz calls it the world of "attainable reach." The actual reality directly before the subject is thus embedded into the extension of past and future, albeit in somewhat different ways. Similarly the vivid present is embedded in a spatial extension. Some things are before the subject and others are

*See Alfred Schutz, *Collected Papers,* Volume I, pp. 218-219 op. cit.

placed elsewhere in the spatial map of his environment. The "now" and the "here" of the actual moment of experience are located on our "maps" of time and space and thereby related to things which we know of elsewhere on these maps.

The second context is that of symbolism and symbolic possibility. The actual reality before us is symbolically but one of all possible constellations. The actual world, of course, can be imagined in different ways because it can be subsumed under a variety of general types. These alternatives may be desirable or undesirable, probable or improbable, the point here is only that they can be conceived. This is what Lewin and others have called the "irreality level". The actually given experience of the moment is embedded in this context because it conforms to the same rules of symbolic consistency and symbolic transformation which apply to all possible worlds (even though we may be capable of operating under a multiplicity of such rules). The actual reality, if seriously experienced, will exclude the symbolically possible alternatives; it will be placed in relation to other possibilites. In the modality of symbolization this extension covers the range from concrete imagery to the emptiness of pure formalization in mathematics and from the lived "reality" to dreamlike "unreality".

The third extension is that of values. One can incorporate the same given actuality into a variety of possible value perspectives. For example, in a group of people looking at a forest, a tourist might enjoy the beauty of the trees, a lumber man might calculate the net profit on the timber, a hiker might look for campsites, and an artist might view it in still another way. The value perspectives may incorporate the same actuality into different contexts and thus give it quite different specific meanings, even though there is no doubt that it is the same actuality.

In the contexts of values, symbolization, and space-time the placing of experienced actuality in different ways may give rise to several different types of meaningfully interpreted reality. Such interpretation may be almost entirely private, at least from the perspective of the experiencing individual. We may even value the very privacy of a certain experience, the knowledge that it is ours alone; and yet the decision to keep it to ourselves links the experienced actuality to the communicative context; we place it in relation to channels of communication by deciding to keep it to ourselves as well as by informing others about it.

The actually encountered reality acquires here a social dimension. The rules of communication in society define the pathways through which one may move from the "world within my reach" to the "world within his reach", the other's reach. We are quite willing to accept the reality of things which we have never seen when they are communicated to us through socially and culturally defined channels. Yet we only accept communicated reality under certain conditions. We have, for instance, one set of conditions defining the communicability of scientific knowledge, another set defining the communicability of religious knowledge, still another for political knowledge, and so on.

The fact that others know reality is something which we never doubt; communication puts the "world in their reach" within our reach, too. A crucial prototype of this process occurs in person-to-person interaction. Here, in the direct communication between two people who attend to each other fully and speak the same language, the shared vivid present of the "We" establishes shared reality. However, this model of communication is restricted when we shift our attention from face-to-face communication to institutional networks of social roles. Social roles establish limited and conditional domains of "We" experiences.

The fourth extension of the experienced reality of things, then, is also an important one. It consists of the linkage of the reality construct to relevant channels of communication. Since society is based on the effectiveness of communication and requires the actual solution of shared problems, the cultural standardization and social control of communicated reality constructs becomes a crucial matter. It is so effective and "natural," in fact, that the very idea of social mechanisms controlling the perception and the communication of the reality of experienced things is quite repulsive to most of us. And yet, our own tendencies to rely on the word of some others, to accept the advice of specialists, to credit or disregard the reports of some journalists are examples of some such mechanisms. There are social patterns in the distribution of doubt and acceptance resulting in channels of communities of communication. These, in turn, influence the way in which members of a society may know reality as much as they represent an important aspect of social structure itself.

If the immediately given reality is apprehended by us as meaningful by being placed into the different basic contexts of time-space, of symbolism, of values, and of communication, it receives further interpretation, at least potentially, by being ordered in relation to other information in terms of a more specific frame of reference which is considered relevant to it. Through such further interpretation a symbolic expression of the experienced reality may be related to theories, which are believed to explain that type of event. Reality experience is symbolically transformed within a frame of reference into knowledge of reality, which now may enter explicitly into a communication channel relevant to it. "Knowledge" we must define as the communicable mapping of some aspect of experience by an observer in terms of a symbolic system and frame of reference deemed relevant and appropriate. It may then be subject to methodical treatment and symbolic transformations. Each person has at his command a large variety of such frames of reference, of theories, of methodologies; he can approach reality not only within the four broad contexts of immediate experience, but he is capable of a variety of specific interpretations of it.

The simple givenness of reality for the natural attitude assumes now an unsuspected complexity. Taking a somewhat closer look, we recognize that there are many different levels and layers of reality experience. The large variation in modes of interpretation adds further to the diversity of domains of reality for any given individual person.

Multiple Realities: The Diversity of Reality in Social Life

An adult, in conversation with a young child, may easily discover that the child's experience of the reality before both of them differs very much from his own. Not only are different things important to the child because of his different vital concerns, but the child also may categorize these things in different ways, and he may hold quite seriously theories about them which to the adult appear absurd. The adult's world is far more differentiated, and he deals with his knowledge in different ways; his methods of interpreting and explaining events are likely to be richer and more powerful than those of the child. He can, however, understand at least in outline just how the child perceives a situation; his understanding encompasses the beliefs of the child, even though he does not share them. On this basis he may guide the child directly or indirectly; his understanding gives him power over the child.

A different case of such differentiation is that of the expert and the common man. The expert presumably has access to reality hidden from the view of others of us in our roles as common men. He has methods and theories vastly more powerful than our "common sense." The expert, however, let us say the lawyer or the engineer, does not need to understand our total mode of viewing the world. We approach him with a "problem" in a more or less clearly defined situation, and we hope and expect that he will be able to solve it for us. We acknowledge the expert as an individual who possesses a frame of reference, methodologies, and a store of knowledge of a specialized nature. He is taken as representative of those who are competent to deal with the problem we have, and we concede to him a considerable degree of power to make decisions for us. The distribution of knowledge, which becomes in the example of our relations with experts such an obviously significant social fact, illustrates the diversity of reality in social life.

Cultural variations may produce the effect of a social distribution of large differences in the experience of reality. The stranger visiting an unknown society may be an example. His view of the reality which he experiences together with his hosts is only in small part shared. As his relationship with his hosts develops, he must, at least for the moment, attempt to understand the others' experiences and their interpretation. In such social interaction he must develop doubt in and distance from his own accustomed definition of reality. In this process, estrangement from his past beliefs, discovery, and reconstruction of new, more encompassing frames of reference are constantly changing phases.

Even a superficial look at the diversity of experienced and interpreted reality in social life shows the complexity of the social distribution of different ways of knowing and different modes of access to reality experience. The social distribution of knowledge or of reality constructs, i.e. of information believed by somebody to represent "facts," emerges as a phenomenon at least equal in importance to the differentiation of experienced "sub-universes" of reality in the mental life of the individual. In fact we may suspect that much of the diversity of reality for the individual may be due to his manifold social participations and the frames of reference offered to him by his social roles.

Reality Shocks

Having explored the diversity of modes of constructing reality in a brief overview of the issue, we may now turn to another issue often obscured by our naive faith in reality. Not only do we tend to believe in the unity of reality, but we also are so convinced of the certitude, the firmness of reality, that to emphasize the point appears trite. And yet there are experiences which show that the seemingly so firm experience of reality may be very fragile; we discover that our firm confidence in known reality requires elaborate supports of which we are usually entirely unaware.

There are psychopathological borderline cases of persons who are deprived of their sense of reality. While they continue to perceive things as others perceive them, they are unable to affix to their percepts the existential quality: "these things are real." They speak of the dreamlike feeling of unreality, encompassing not only things but themselves, their own existence and beliefs. Such states can be induced by drugs, and at times they may afflict the normal person. In the normal life of the individual there do occur certain moments where we have the feeling "this is not real." It is the feeling "I've got to pinch my "self" to see if I am really here. In these moments the person is jolted out of the natural attitude which we all share when we accept without any further question "the cold facts as they are." We will call these experiences "reality shocks," the unanticipated feeling of unreality arising in situations of extreme disappointment or extreme success, or in situations in which the social support for our interpretation of reality is withdrawn, or in which we are confronted by entirely meaningless events. The consideration of reality shocks is of particular importance, showing that the borderline between the firm, solid territory of everyday reality and the realm of unreality is at times quite thin.

Sometimes the reality shock may be extremely threatening.

One is compelled, at least momentarily, to adopt a stance of utter doubt toward the natural attitude and toward natural reality. In fact, reality may collapse, and it must then be reconstructed in a sometimes frantic search for an appropriate new perspective. The stubborn denial of evidence may be one of the means of defense open in the situation. Let us consider the case in which something believed to be "impossible" occurs. It may be the fact of defeat of his nation for the ardent patriot. The story is told that in a few isolated cases among members of certain Japanese sects, the fact of Japan's defeat in World War II is even today considered to be a pure fabrication of the press, concealing the true state of affairs (Japan's victory) from the public. We are also told that the psychological defense (here reality denial) arose out of deep cries and states of utter confusion. The "impossible" event (impossible relative to firmly held theories about the state of the world) occurred and caused the reality shock of disappointment. By contrast to this shock of frustration, Durkheim has given us in his descriptions of anomic states many illustrations of the breakdown of orientation and grasp of reality which may also be a consequence of extreme success. The frame of reference of the suddenly successful person is upset, the limits of the possible and the impossible become blurred and a severe, possibly suicidal disturbance of the person may result.

The utter doubt and confusion characteristic of reality shock may merely be the result of finding oneself at variance with the perceptions of others. The sharedness of physical perception and of the interpretation of what we see, is so much an unquestioned basis of our actions that the withdrawal of social support can cause threat and confusion. We may think of the illustration provided by the experiments of Solomon Asch, in which he instructed a number of confederates to disagree systematically with the judgments of one or more "naive," uninitiated subjects on the length of some clearly different lines.* The doubt and confusion which many subjects reported when they heard apparently reasonable people contradict the clear evidence of their senses is a case in point. Examples of the sometimes devastating effect of the withdrawal of social support

*S. E. Asch, "Effects of group pressure upon the modification and distortion of judgment" in H. Guetzkow, ed. Groups, Leadership and Men, Pittsburgh, Carnegie Press, 1951.

for the interpretation of reality in situatiòns of practical importance come even more readily to mind. Changes in political and religious convictions as a consequence of changes in group membership and group-identification of a person find their explanation.

The confrontation with the meaningless event, for example the accident or disaster which breaks into a well-ordered social world and destroys its certainties, may serve as a final example of the conditions which can bring about reality shocks. The initial phase of disbelief, of consternation and bewilderment, may be overcome by recourse to non-empirical, religious theories which endow the event, meaningless in itself, with some meaning after the fact.

The meaning structures of everyday life define the world in which we are confident and in which we are at home. When we are confronted by their limitations, anxiety arises, either in the sudden panic of a crisis or in the nagging, persistent anxiety that something unknown is drastically wrong. Each one of the severe reality shocks represents such a crisis in which we experience the limitations of our meaning-structures.

Less fundamental threats, but still important ones, arise from the problem of dealing with uncertainties. Every decision maker is faced by the problem of uncertainty inherent in the lack of knowledge about, or in the known unpredictability of the environment in which he acts. The amount of uncertainty to be dealt with probably increases with an increasing rate of social change, but the problem exists in all societies. Techniques for the handling of uncertainty are developed which supposedly reduce it to manageable scope. There does always remain an irreducible residue, however, and the possibility exists that the failure to control uncertainty, or an especially low tolerance for uncertainty, may produce reality shocks.

Experienced and interpreted, structured reality is now exposed as bounded by confusion and meaninglessness; known reality is structured and limited. The maintenance of reality experience, and of meaning structures is a most delicate process involving social supports for preferred modes of reality perception. While reality is phenomenologically experienced as simply given and "there," we now understand that this is not unproblematic. In the context of social life the various experiences of reality must be recognized as socially maintained constructions.

UNIVERSITY LIBRARIES
CARNEGIE-MELLON UNIVERSITY
PITTSBURGH, PENNSYLVANIA 15213

The Discovery and the Construction of Reality

For our naive, unreflected experience the reality we know is discovered, not constructed. But our second, more reflective look, teaches us that even perceptions of physical things are structured by living concerns, are influenced by our mapping of time and space, our symbolic patterns, our values, and our communicative links. The emergent experience begins to take on meaning for us in these different contexts. It is placed in relation to other, already meaningful experiences and in relation to ourselves. This means the emergent experience must be interpreted before it becomes knowledge.

To some extent we can vary our interpretation, depending on the frame of reference and the theories which we apply to it. For example, when we see a handsome dog, we may simply appreciate the beauty of the animal. But after we are told by an expert that this dog is a specimen of an especially rare variety, and after the expert calls our attention to the details of the dog's eyes, ears, tail and the like, the interpretation of what we have seen changes. Some information about the dog even escaped our notice before. Because we did not share the expert's "preference system" we had no reason to attend, preferentially, to these items. The whole frame of reference into which we now place the dog we see is a quite different one from before.

Frames of reference influence our perception, but even more they influence our interpretation of what we see, and the formulation of plans of action. Given a frame of reference, which directs our attention to a particular range of possible experiences, and equips us with methods of relating what we find to other knowledge, we do indeed feel that we discover reality, since we cannot vary our perceptions at will. Yet, we can vary the frame of reference and discover still different aspects of the actuality before us. It is, then, useful to describe the cognitive process as if it were an active process of reality construction on the part of the experiencing subject. When, finally, we formulate in some symbolic system or language what we have experienced, the resulting symbolic representation contains the residues of so many active transformations of the original experience, that we are entirely justified in calling it a "reality construct."

The word "reality construct" will be used throughout this book. It may appear to some unnecessarily cumbersome. We wish to defend it on the grounds that we need the term. It indicates that we are not concerned with the study of ideal conditions for the discovery of truly "objective facts" as such. This means that we do not search for normative grounds on which to defend the superiority of any particular perspective such as that of science. Instead, we study descriptively the conditions under which social agents of different kinds consider any information as representing a "fact." This implies that for the purposes of our discussion we must bracket the question of the objective validity of any of these alleged facts of reality constructs; we are concerned with the social processes of reality construction, and we study and "discover" them from the perspective of the sociologist.

The process of reality construction cannot be conceptualized as a mechanical sequence of events. Reality constructs are formed in the interpretation and re-interpretation of experience. Still, we will be able to analyze the process into some of its essential components or aspects. In doing so, we may follow to a certain extent the work done by psychologists and by phenomenologists. But we will never forget that the construction of reality occurs in a social context; we must transcend the phenomenology of it until we reach a sociology of reality construction. Only then can we hope to understand the reasons for the wide divergence in modes of reality construction, which can lead different persons to make sometimes entirely different assertions about the "same" state of affairs (as seen by some third observer).

Each person in his social setting approaches the environment in which he moves with a limited and a specific repertory of frames of reference or orientations. These orientations are in limited supply and not infinitely variable; they are found in a patterned distribution within a structured social system. Such a distribution of orientations we will call the "orientational structure" of society. At the same time we find that society limits and distributes the chances of acces to actual situations, to physical environments. Society can be seen as a vast allocative mechanism, regulating the access to different types of environments which different types of persons are likely to have. We will call the distribution of access to environments the "situational structure" (but with some misgivings about the possible ambiguities of the term). The social distributions of modes of reality construction and the distribution of the resulting "reality constructs" is likely to be a consequence of the complex interactions among these two distinct aspects of the social system. What an individual is likely to encounter in his environment must be seen as regulated by the allocative mechanisms of society; it is patterned by the situational structure into which he is placed. How he will interpret and communicate his experience is, in turn, a consequence of his frames of reference or orientations.

The Problems of the Sociology of Knowledge

We are, it is clear, dealing with problems of the sociology of knowledge. But it is necessary to redefine these problems. One of the dominant concerns in the sociology of knowledge was the analysis of the "problem of ideology," usually the sociological debunking of a set of assertions. This approach to the sociology of knowledge is concisely expressed in the onesided and doctrinaire assertion of Karl Marx and Friedrich Engels in *The German Ideology*: ". . . we do not set out from what men say, imagine, conceive, nor from men as narrated, thought of, imagined, conceived, in order to arrive at men in the flesh. We set out from real, active men, and on the basis of their real life process we demonstrate the development of the ideological reflexes and echoes of this life process. The phantoms formed in the human brain are also, necessarily, sublimates of their material life process, which is empirically verifiable and bound to material premises. Morality, religion, metaphysics, all the rest of ideology and their corresponding forms of consciousness thus no longer retain the semblance of independence. They have no history, no development; but men, developing their material production, and their material intercourse, alter, along with this, their real existence, their thinking, and products of their thinking. Life is not determined by consciousness, but consciousness by life. In the first method of approach the starting point is consciousness, taken as the living individual; in the second it is the real, living individuals themselves, as they are in actual life, and consciousness is considered solely as their consciousness."*

There is, in this paragraph, an admirable expression of the social scientist's passion to grasp the "reality" of social life.

*Karl Marx and Friedrich Engels, *The German Ideology*.

There is a profound respect for the power and grandeur of "actual life" in contrast to the disdain Marx and Engels have for the dried up, shriveled, artificial world of intellectual constructions. The trouble is, of course, that this dualism between "actual life" and "ideologies" or "reality" and "phantoms" is vastly oversimplified, and it left Marx and Engels in a rather frightful conceptual muddle. It is not at all clear why men's thoughts and ideas should be "less real" than their material life, nor is it at all clear what is involved in explaining ideas or systems of ideas in terms of "material life processes." What men "say, imagine, conceive" is, after all, very much a part of "real life."

European sociology has treated the topic of the relationship between ideas and social processes as its central concern for decades. Weber, Durkheim, Pareto, and Simmel, each in his own way, tackled the problem of the interrelations between ideas and beliefs on one side, and observable social structures on the other. There is no need to review their well-known works here, nor is it necessary to pause to acquaint the reader with the important classic formulations of the sociology of knowledge by Max Scheler and Karl Mannheim. The contemporary sociologist knows these works, but it seems that he has abandoned an interest in their comprehensive problems. At least we should say that the sociology of knowledge was almost abandoned until the recent resurgence of interest. Its problems appeared to be too vague and too elusive to fit the criteria and standards of behavioral empiricism. And it is true enough that there are several major objections to the classic formulations of the sociology of knowledge which owe so much to Max Scheler, criticisms among which there are three which appear to us especially telling.

In the first place, there was the tendency to construct an interpretation of social change in terms of a questionable dualism between "Geist" and "Leben," between "ideas" and "real life." This metaphysical dualism is dangerously misleading since it constructs presumably mutually exclusive categories which, however, can be shown to overlap and interpenetrate. In the second place, there was a tendency to work with gross variables only, such as "social classes," or "stages of history." One may suppose that this preference for rather coarse sociological variables made the maintenance of the metaphysical dualism possible. It collapses, if one takes a closer look. Finally, there is the third issue, frequently commented upon, which concerns the highly questionable epistemologies on which the sociologies of knowledge by Durkheim, Scheler, and Mannheim were based. We do not wish to dwell especially on the methodological argument that the European sociology of knowledge was "speculative," because we do not regard it as an argument of principle: "speculation" must be welcomed in empirical science if it organizes or explains empirical knowledge, or leads to its extension in the future.

In an attempt at redefining the problems of the sociology of knowledge, we will have to be limited and we must depart from at least some traditions. There are three problem areas which we can list: 1) the socio-cultural processes which shape the construction of reality; 2) the effects of modes of reality construction on the social structure; 3) the distribution of reality constructs in the social structure.

We do know a number of important things about the socio-cultural processes which influence the construction of reality in the person. This is largely the domain of a cognitive social psychology which attempts to explain how the reality construct, i.e. the symbolically articulated reality experience, arises. The social psychology of orientations and modes of symbolization can give us important insights. We must also consider in this connection the sociology of the allocation of situations (environments) to persons; clearly the regularities in actual experiences are as important as a person's orientation to them.

The second domain of problems is quite complex. Here the sociology of knowledge must concern itself with the fact that social structure channels interaction into patterns, which themselves are co-determined by the reality constructs which the participants hold or evolve. Modes of reality construction enter with other determinants of the interaction process into the shaping of social structure itself. Images of society, social beliefs, images of other persons are elements in this process.

The third problem area again is vast, but it offers methodologically the least resistance to the inquiring sociologist. It deals with the patterned distribution and control of knowledge in a society. The differentiation of social roles means also the differentiation of frames of reference and of knowledge; communication patterns exist with the effect of distributing certain kinds of knowledge only to certain kinds of people. The distributed knowledge is made available for social action in a variety of ways, for example by "referral" of a client or of a problem to an expert. There are distinct sociological reasons for the maintenance and for the shift of patterns of knowledge distribution which are very much in need of investigation. In fact, we suggest that this problem area should become the central concern of an empirically oriented sociology of knowledge which can explore the social distribution and social control of modes of reality construction and of different types of reality constructs.

That these three problem areas are difficult, we will not deny. But we do believe that they, and especially the third, are amenable to the approaches of non-evaluative social science, whereas much of the sociology of knowledge of the Scheler and Marx traditions must remain a matter for admittedly important evaluative debate, which is outside our frame of reference.

The next four chapters in Part I will address themselves to the issues in the first two problem areas, the determinants of the process of reality construction, and the effects of modes of reality construction on social structure. Part II of this essay is concerned with the different aspects of the distribution of reality constructs in the social structure. It explores the third and central domain of the sociology of knowledge. In Part III we will concentrate on the social organization of two major modes of reality construction; it deals with the social organization and distribution of specialized working knowledge and with that of ideological knowledge.

Chapter II

Observations on the Structure of Cognitive Activity

Knowledge as Reality Constructs

Cognitive action is that activity which is primarily concerned with the gaining and communication of knowledge. An understanding of the components of this type of action is needed for our further work. We might profitably begin this task with a reflection on some elementary epistemological facts. The results of philosophical investigation at least since the time of Immanuel Kant show that "knowledge" can only mean the "mapping" of experienced reality by some observer. It cannot mean the "grasping" of reality itself. In fact, philosophical progress has produced the conclusive insight that there can be no such thing as the direct and "true" apprehension of "reality" itself. More strictly speaking, we are compelled to define "knowledge" as the communicable mapping of some aspect of experienced reality by an observer in symbolic terms.

This definition is more than an arbitrary definition of a mere word; it is, we argue, the only possible definition of "knowledge" that has any meaning at all. It implies that knowledge by its very nature is relational. It emerges in the relationship between the observer and the reality which he observes, as the result of mapping operations. The observer plots, so to speak, what he sees in terms of some set of rules that define what is a permissible map.

One may use explicitly the analogy of the cartographer. He proceeds quite concretely in this way. When he designs a map of some geographical area, he does not create a reproduction of "reality" itself. He does not even aim at an approximation of the "full grasping" of reality. On the contrary he has a number of pre-established rules which both provide the enabling basis and important constraints for his work. One set of rules would be concerned with the scale of the map and the type of projection to be used. Another would be concerned with the type of symbols to be used to indicate cities and towns and mountains. Still others would be concerned with the relationships among the objects represented on the map. The knowledge which the cartographer obtains and represents through his map is a projection of what he has observed onto a pre-established network of categories and coordinates, in terms of which he selects and arranges his observations.

It can be shown that these principles hold for all types of human knowledge. They permit us to specify certain important issues in the study of knowledge. In the first place the observer, relating himself to "reality," must select from among all humanly possible perspectives one perspective in terms of which he approaches this particular reality before him. Most often the selection of a cognitive perspective is made implicitly, without conscious choice; in part it may be dictated by the noncognitive, e.g. the physical, or the personal relation of the observer to his object. Let us use the analogy of an aerial photograph: one must know the perspective determined by the relative location of camera and objects in order to assess the meaning of the information captured by the film.

Secondly, beyond the definition of the perspective, the knowing observer must abide by certain rules of mapping which are essentially given by the structure of the symbolic system which he uses. The nature of the concepts, the nature of the permissible operations with these concepts, is in large measure defined by the structure of the symbolic system itself, e.g. by the language in terms of which he describes reality. There are several specific aspects of the structure of symbolic systems significant for "mapping." They are, for example, its internal organization, the relation between the symbols and the experiential referents, and the requirements of communication.

First, there is the internal structure of the symbolic system, itself defining the limitations for the possible forms of knowledge that can be recorded in that "language." Here one finds such restrictions as the disciplines imposed on us by the rules of logic, or by the grammar of the language we speak. These are definitely restrictive rules because logic and grammar permit only certain sentences and do not permit others. What is consistency and contradiction is defined by this internal structuring of the symbolic system itself, so that there must be certain normative principles around which the symbolic system is arranged.

The second aspect of symbolic systems, however, is a little more problematic. The symbolic system does not only specify rules of internal consistency, or rules for the transformation of knowledge within the system, but also specifies the linkages between the symbol and the experience represented. For example, in the symbolic system of science, this is expressed in the problem of concept validity. The question is: how does the symbol become affixed to some observable, experienceable set of events? How does the symbol relate to the realm of direct experience, constitutive meanings? In the last analysis the anchorage of symbols in human experience occurs in the "Erlebnis" of meaning. Accordingly, the problem of concept validity in science is solved originally in a subjective way. This is the reason why methodologists have always had great difficulties in assessing concept validity "objectively." The final basis of validity is simply the subjective experience of "this is evident." There occurs in it a match between conception and perception. It is only in building on this basis that scientific rules can transform subjective experiences into intersubjectively communicable and verifiable meanings.

In the intersubjective framework of science the notion of validity can then assume a more restricted meaning. In the predictive context of scientific work, validity means the magnitude of the correlation between what is being measured and what the measure is intended to predict. This is a highly derived notion which, however, cannot in the last analysis escape its foundation in the experiential matching of concept and percept.

The experience that creates the meaning of a concept itself is a "moment of discovery." A child, for instance, discovers an aspect of reality, labels it, and recognizes this aspect as something that stands out, hangs together within itself, has some internal structure, in short: it is a complex separated out from the rest of the confronted situation, and it is represented by some name. In this "discovery" the link symbol—experience is established.

The third major issue in the general mapping of reality by an observer is concerned with the rules of communication binding on him. "Knowing," described in terms of the first two aspects that were mentioned this far, could be purely personal and individual. It becomes transformed into what common sense calls "knowledge" only by being again restricted and restructured by rules defining the communicability of the resulting "map." Through communication, a third discipline is imposed on the emerging map of an aspect of reality that an observer may construct. He must, essentially, be able to point to what he means in the presence of some second person who, thus sharing his "discovery of meaning," develops the same "map" as our first observer.

The rules of communication have a very important role to play in structuring different types of knowledge, especially notable in the domain of science. The very structure of scientific concepts is affected by the fact that the map of reality defined by them must be communicable in a specific way. In the case of science this is epitomized in the issue of reliability. Reliability requires the establishment of efficient communication among scientific observers through the construction of visible "pointers" to the communicated reality constructs, and the standardization of measurement. Reliability is essentially the pragmatic test of observer standardization by demonstrating the practical interchangeability of observers within the communication network of science. Other, non-scientific patterns of specialized knowledge also deal with the problem of reliable communication of reality experiences, but in a multiplicity of different ways.

In summary, then: knowledge is always the knowledge of an observer and therefore inescapably relational in nature. There is no absolute access to what Kant called a "thing in itself." The nature of this relationality is defined by the observer's perspective or frame of reference, the structure of the symbolic system he uses, its anchorage in his experience, and by the rules that specify particular ways and channels of communicating the resulting meanings to others; all of this necessarily reflected in the theories or "Maps" of reality which he forms.

The Behavior and the Experience of Perceiving

Psychology has achieved a considerable amount of agreement on the nature of the perceptual process. There is no conflict between these findings and the epistemological view of knowledge formation as a process of mapping. First, and important above all, is the recognition that perception is indeed a process, an activity of the subject. There has been a convergence of findings on this issue, obtained by quite different psychological "schools," such as the holistic psychology of Friedrich Sander and the behavioristic approach of Edward C. Tolman.

Secondly, it has been recognized that the perceptual process evolves through a number of more or less distinct stages of varying degrees of "vulnerability" to extraneous influences, that is, to factors not directly connected with the immediate relation subject-stimulus. Certainty, as a subjective state of confidence in one's perception, is likely to arise only at the very end of the process.

Using the classification of perceptual stages offered by Solley and Murphy* — albeit somewhat loosely — we can say that the following phases must be distinguished, while keeping in mind that each of them relates the whole person in a particular way to the perceptual act: 1) the expectation of stimulation, 2) the focusing of attention, 3) the reception of the stimulus, 4) the interplay of trial and check, along with autonomic and proprioceptive arousal and feedback, and ultimately, 5) the final structuring of the percept, particularly along "natural lines," such as figure-ground articulation.

The first phase consists essentially of the sensitization of the organism to certain aspects of the environment and the formation of an expectation of stimulation. Some writers refer to the establishment of "sets" at this point. The expectancy prepares the organism for the fine tuning of selective attention to the stimulus which constitutes the second phase. While the expectancy of the first phase establishes a range of possible attention now, in the second phase, there forms a narrow and specific focus. The third stage is that of "reception." Even the original

*Charles M. Solley and Gardner Murphy, *Development of the Perceptual World*, Basic Books, New York, 1960.

reception, and not only the interpretation of the stimulus, will differ somewhat depending on the frame of reference that the organism has built up. Whether the water in a bath tub, for instance, is hot or cold depends on the person's general state of expectancy; in this case upon the previous experience of the person, e.g., in a hot, tropical day or in a wintry, cold one. Whether something is "dark" or "bright" depends again on the adaptation level of the eyes.

Upon the first reception there follows the complex phase of "trial and check." Other writers have described this process as the construction of "hypotheses" by the subject. The subject attempts to match a variety of symbolically defined hypotheses with the stimulus. He sees "something," but he cannot immediately identify what it is, except by looking for some distinguishing marks that would, if present, verify his guess as to what it might be. The nature of the early guesses will largely depend on the state of the subject, that is, his various preoccupations at the moment. Obviously, his guesses about a not yet clearly apprehended stimulus-object will differ if he anticipates a strongly hoped for or an intensely feared event. One may think of the mysterious creaking in the dark house at night which may be interpreted as the step of a member of the family on the stairs, as the involuntarily produced sign of a sneaking burglar, now standing and holding his breath to see if he aroused the household, or as the movement of the house in adjusting to changing temperature, or as the working of a "poltergeist." Surely we have not exhausted the possibilities of the example, but the point is clear: the nature of the sound itself is not enough to account for the guesses formed. Solley and Murphy speak of "autonomic and proprioceptive arousal and feedback" in their discussion of this stage: the formation of "guesses" or "hypotheses" depends in very high measure upon the processes taking place within the person himself.

The final structuring of the percept emerges out of the whole process. It is, of course, constrained by the symbolic definition of the object and its natural characteristics, such as boundaries or contrasts. We see, for instance, a table as a unified object, all of its parts belonging together. If we did not know better, why should we not, instead, see the table legs as protrusions of the floor and the table top as merely an independent, flat object put on top of them? Where the boundaries between objects run, therefore, depends on our previous knowledge and the symbolic definition of the thing itself.

In this highly vulnerable process of perception, various "distortions" can easily intrude. With some puzzlement we must then ask the psychologist how "veridical," that is, undistorted, "truthful" perception is possible. He can give, at the very best, a partial answer. Perception is "veridical" if we can obtain intersubjective agreement on its content by some direct or indirect method. Its most primitive basis rests in the fact of the similarities in the perceptual equipment biologically given in the human species. We simply do not perceive in the way spiders, bees, or crocodiles perceive, but in our own, peculiarly human way. We are sensitive to certain wave lengths of light, of sound, and only to these wave lengths. This, however, is too broad and basic a fact to account for the "veridical" perception of culturally defined objects, which requires us to accept the importance of cognitive socialization and the social control of orientations for the "proper" preparation of the observer.

The description of behaviorally different stages is essentially matched by the phenomenological description of the experiential process of perceiving, in which the object emerges out of a broad perceptual field. The emergence of the object and the restructuring of the field as a result of interpretive recognition of what is seen is nicely illustrated in the following example given by Merleau-Ponty: "If I walk along a shore towards a ship which has run aground, and the funnel or masts merge into the forest bordering on the sand dune, there will be a moment when these details suddenly become part of the ship, and indissolubly fused with it. As I approached, I did not perceive resemblances or proximities which finally came together to form a continuous picture of the upper part of the ship. I merely felt that the look of the object was on the point of altering, that something was imminent in this tension, as a storm is imminent in storm clouds. Suddenly the sight before me was recast in a manner satisfying my vague expectation. Only afterwards did I recognize, as justifications for the change, the resemblance and contiguity of what I call 'stimuli' — namely the determinate phenomena, seen at close quarters and with which I compose the 'true' world. 'How could I have failed to see that these pieces of wood were an integral part of the ship? For they were of the same colour as the ship, and fitted well enough into its superstructure.' But these reasons for correct perception were not given as reasons beforehand. The unity of the object is based on the foreshadowing of an imminent order which is about to spring upon us a reply to questions merely latent in the landscape. It solves a problem set only in the form of a vague feeling of uneasiness, it organizes elements which up to that moment did not belong to the same universe and which, for that reason, as Kant said with profound insight, could not be associated. By placing them on the same footing, that of the unique object, synopsis makes continuity and resemblance between them possible. An impression can never by itself be associated with another impression."*

Both the findings of behavioral psychology and the description of the experiential process of object perception by the phenomenologist establish the process nature of perception and point to its basis in motivationally founded expectations. In the course of this process there occurs an interaction between sense experience and symbolization. Linking the present discussion with our previous remarks about the basic contexts of the moment of actual experience, we can say that as the process of perception and interpretation progresses, the percept or phenomenon becomes more and more precisely located in the contexts of time-space, symbolization, values, and communicative potential. It is finally subject to definite interpretation in the terms of a more or less specific frame of reference. The stage sequence of progressive clarification may include a phase of vascillation, of back-and-forth movement between different interpretations of what is seen, further perception, until the final interpretation is arrived at. It is important to note that the process of perception is in a sense a process of discovery as well as one of construction: each tentative interpretation or recognition of the object is a discovery of new information, but it also

*Maurice Merleau-Ponty, *Phenomenology of Perception,* translated by Colin Smith, The Humanities Press, New York, 1962, p. 17.

is a construction in the sense of involving a general restructuring of the scene before us, definite selection of information from what is perceptually given, and the unification of information into conceptually representable objects and relations.

The Symbolic Stabilization of the Perceived World

Our orientation to reality and our interpretation of it develops with the growth of our personality, in the context of cognitive socialization. In the process distinct stages of cognitive organization and of consequently different modes of reality interpretation can be distinguished. The stages proceed from the relatively unstable meaning-complexes of earliest childhood to the symbolically stabilized and interpreted world. In order to understand the structure of different modes of reality construction, and especially the functions of symbolism in this process, a schematic review of the cognitive development of personality is now required. Our discussion will be based on the work of such authors as Jean Piaget, Erik H. Erikson, Charles M. Solley, Gardner Murphy and others, in a necessarily simplified and abritrary fashion. Our purpose must be to understand the major transformations in modes of reality constructions through cognitive socialization.

In order to define, at least roughly, the beginnings of development, we look at the situation of the unsocialized, very young infant. We find an organism endowed with certain innate behavioral capacities and tendencies. Relevant to our understanding of the socialization of cognition is the innate perceptual apparatus given in the structure of the sense organs and the nervous system. Primitive perceptual mechanisms are those of selective attention, contour formation, contrast, and figure—ground differentiation. By "selective attention" we mean the capability of a child to follow, for instance, a glittering object at least for a short period of time, a few seconds at first. It means that he is capable of focusing on something, separating it from the rest of the environment as something which stands out. This capacity is a necessary prerequisite of all learning, in that the acquisition of association and the development of cognitive structures requires the discrimination and selective perception of some information first. Responses always have a discriminatory aspect. The other perceptual mechanisms of contour and contrast formation, of primitive figure-ground differentiation, can be viewed simply as contributory to the selective attention mechanisms.

If we try to describe phenomenologically the way in which a small child probably experiences his situations, we are forced to recognize it as a flow of sensations and percepts in which there is no continuity and stability of objects. The unity of the child's experiential field, that is of the totality of his experiences at any moment, rests on the unity of his emotions and actions. At this stage emotional states become generalized to "color" the whole field of experiences. With shifting emotions and their underlying motives, there is a change in cognitions.

This feature can be characterized as primitive autism in the child; it is his restriction to the emotional and self centered unity of the experiential field. While the experiential field is emotionally unified, at any moment, it is constantly fleeting, changing. We may observe this process directly in a small infant, in the way in which his whole body gives expression to his emotional states. The same state of affairs is described differently by pointing out that his various sensory fields are not cognitively integrated. We may speak of different "sensory spaces" within which the child cognizes his situation. Such sensory spaces, of which the space of touch in various body regions, of smell, of sight, of sound, of taste, are examples, are differentiated. An object passing from one of these sensory spaces into another appears, for the child, to change its nature. The same object calls up responses from the child which are entirely distinct, depending on the sensory space in which he perceives the object. We arrive at the conclusion that, in fact, for the very small infant the bottle as seen is not the same "thing" as the felt or tasted bottle. Within these sensory or perceptual spaces, then, there is a constant flow of disconnected and unstable experiences. There is almost no permanence or stability in the perceptual world of the infant.

How does cognitive patterning arise out of this seeming chaos? It involves above all the gradual crystallization of stable complexes of meanings. Out of the flow of experiences certain clusters of meanings come to be separated from others, are surrounded by a boundary, and develop an internal structure.

Primarily, this occurs through experiences of the child in the manipulation of things.

Through manipulating things, objects, the child learns the principle of equivalence between different sensory spaces. "Equivalence" has a very concrete meaning here: one and the same activity spans several sensory spaces and establishes a cluster of meanings (e.g. bottle-grasping-sucking-satisfaction), cutting through several of them. It remains a cluster of meaningful experience limited to the immediate present, and restricted to the narrow boundaries of action. Gradually, through the integration of the schematic organization of action across the different sensory fields, there emerges a coalescence of originally separate meaning structures. A child may see an object, grasp it, move it, and put it into his mouth. There are complicated acts of learning and cognition involved in this seemingly simple performance; the child has to recognize this object from other visual stimuli, he grasps it and thereby it becomes incorporated into the sensory space of touch, changing its experienced quality altogether. At first the experiential qualities of this one and the same object in the different sensory spaces are so distinct that the child does not make the connection between them. He learns, through the continuity of the manipulation, with its grasping, moving, putting into mouth, sucking, and other aspects, that there is coherence in the act-object. Thus arise bounded clusters of meaning which cut across different sensory spaces in manipulation.

The point is well illustrated by Piaget in his description of the development of visual "schemas" or meaning structures: "Thus it may be said that, independently of any coordination between vision and other schemata (prehension, touch, etc.) the visual schemata are organized among themselves and constitute more or less well-coordinated totalities. But the essential thing for this immediate question is the coordination of the visual schemata, no longer among themselves, but with the other schemata. Observation shows that very early, perhaps from the very beginnings of orientation in looking, coordination exists between vision and hearing . . . Subsequently the relationships between vision and sucking appear . . . then between vision and prehension, touch, kinesthetic impressions, etc.

These intersensorial coordinations, this organization of hetero-geneous schemata will give the visual images increasingly rich meanings and make visual assimilation no longer an end in itself but an instrument at the service of vaster assimilations. When the child seven or eight months old looks at unknown objects for the first time before swinging, rubbing, throwing and catching them, etc., he no longer tries to look for the sake of looking (pure visual assimilation in which the object is a simple aliment for looking), nor even for the sake of seeing (generalizing or recognitory visual assimilation in which the object is incorporated without adding anything to the already elaborated visual schemata), but he looks in order to act, that is to say, in order to assimilate the new object to the schemata of weighing, friction, falling, etc. There is therefore no longer only assimilation inside the visual schemata but between those and all the others. It is this progressive organization which endows the visual images with their meanings and solidifies them in inserting them in a total universe."*

At this early phase there exists one type of cognitive stabil-ity and organization. It consists solely in the manipulative or-ganization of the act. Only within the boundaries of a gradually established, schematic organization of activity is there integra-tion of the sensory spaces and of meanings. The object which is a potential part of the action schema may possess a meaning for him which is different from the socially assigned meaning of the adult world; it is relative to the child's patterns of activity. Only gradually is the stability of the object beyond the time span of activity recognized by the child, and only gradually does he assign to it meanings shared by others; this process occurs in the context of the social channeling of his activities. The forma-tion of object schemata is a great step forward in the stabiliza-tion of perceived reality.

Here lies also the beginning of the differentiation between "self" and "thing." In the action schema, the thing which the child handles is simply a component of the bounded and

---

*Jean Piaget, *The Origins of Intelligence in Children*. New York, Inter. University Press, 1952, pp. 75-76, quoted after John H. Flavell, *The Devel-opmental Psychology of Jean Piaget,* Toronto, New York, London, Van Nostrand, 1963, p. 57.

experienced cluster of meanings. It is not juxtaposed to the self, is not an "object" to the person. In the next stage of cognitive organization, the "thing," that is the object component of the act, acquires a relative independence of its own because the child learns that it can perform a variety of such manipulatory acts with one and the same thing, incorporating the thing into various clusters of experienced meanings. As soon as this phase develops, there appears the beginning of subject-object differentiation and it is in this stage that the foundations of symbolic learning are laid. Such learning, of course, begins considerably before a child acquires language, because there are important forms of pre-symbolic communication and representation which provide the basis for the acquisition of cultural symbols.

The integration of object meanings beyond the boundaries of simple action schemata and across sensory spaces occurs because of the experienced resistance of the object to attempted manipulation. The child learns that objects follow, as Piaget puts it, their own "trajectories." Objects behave in ways that are defined by natural law and they cannot be made to behave differently; they offer resistance to the manipulatory attempts of the child. Through this resistance the child is "thrown back upon himself"; he is frustrated in his original attempt. But if he is sufficiently motivated to continue his trials, he moves necessarily both into the further exploration of the environment in a different way and an exploration of his self in contrast to the environment. There now emerge object schemata, that is images of objects which are generalized beyond the boundaries of a simple action schema. Object schemata can be symbolically fixed: it is at this stage that symbolic learning accelerates rapidly and leads to the forming of object concepts.

In the case of perception in terms of object-concepts the person does not merely perceive the stimulus itself, but he perceives largely what he knows the stimulus to be. Children who are just learning to speak acquire a way of perceiving the object through labelling it and giving it a name. In the phase of developed object concepts we see that objects as they are perceived are partially constituted by symbolically defined knowledge. The most primitive example would be the instance in which the child claims that he sees what he knows about the object. Children draw, for example, the famous stereotypical pictures of people in profile that have two eyes and two ears on one side, because they know very well that people have two eyes and ears and not just one of each.

Symbolically defined object constancy enables the person to perceive things in a stable framework. The objects thus perceived are in juxtaposition to the self: the mode of experiencing objects implies a mode of experiencing selfhood. The stages in the development of children, from the naive "autism" to the fully mature, "responsible" person, are characterized by differences in the cognitive organization of "objects" and corresponding differences in the modality of "selfhood." Objects thus imply subjects, and changes in subjects mean changes in the experienced object.

Since object concepts are symbolically defined, the perceptual world is already regulated in terms of the symbolic system which the adult person has acquired. This is probably one of the best documented points of the contemporary psychology of perception. The discovery that the adult person does not perceive "sensations" as classical associationists believed, but that he perceives objects, meaningful things, quite directly and naively, is fairly recent.

In social perception as well, persons do not normally perceive the exact physical state of the other's face, to infer from it laboriously what he feels, but they perceive the meaning of his culturally (that is symbolically) defined expression directly. The percept is not "flushed face, agitation, harshness of voice:" the percept is "anger." This perception is direct and unreflected. Of course such percepts can be taken apart into their components, they can be analyzed into "sensations," they can be finally checked, and checked again, if they indeed match the concept. But these analytic performances are high achievements of symbolic abstraction that have little to do with the nature of everyday perception.

At this point a more general statement of the functions of symbolism in the context of cognitive action is in order. A symbol, as we use the term, is a fixed means of representing a conception of an intended object or relation. This means that the symbol, in order to be "a fixed means of representation" must be some kind of perceivable object, e.g. sound waves, marks on paper, or the like, which becomes a "carrier of meaning". The meaning itself is the conception or idea which the symbol evokes in the person "reading" it.

Because the symbol stands for a complex of meanings, for example an object, but is not identical with it, it is free from the pressures of immediacy. It transcends the given situation and it points in some ways (through social convention or individual fixation) to standardized conceptions of intended objects, which may be diffuse images or precise concepts. The user of a symbol is capable of calling up such conceptions in the physical absence of the object and in fact, he can create the conception of an object that never existed and never will exist. Symbolization thus makes possible a "realm of meanings" that encompasses, but is not identical with, the meanings concretely experienced in any specific situation.

Symbolically conveyed conceptions are always abstractions of some degree from the concretely given reality experience itself. They are, as Kant would have it, the result of the human synthesis of experience, and involve some selection, stabilization and organization, "stylization" of the experienced material. Symbolic systems also provide relatively stable rules for such stylizations and arrangements. Symbolic transformations usually follow consistent patterns. Granting the possibility of "error," there is a discriminatory aspect defining rules of "right" and "wrong" built into the very structure of all symbolic systems. In the case of language, such rules are spelled out, for instance, by the grammarian and they constitute standards of judgment for appropriate usage of the symbolic system itself.

These rules for the operation of symbolic systems themselves structure and limit the realm of the symbolically possible. The actually experienced world thus merely represents a special case of those states of affairs which could be symbolically represented, and it is normally a special case of the narrower range of states of affairs which, according to prevailing theories, can be thought of as possible. The opening up of a realm of possibilities and probabilities enhances further the flexibility of the observer's stance towards what he experiences as actual.

The rule structure of the symbolic system thus becomes an important determinant of thought. Benjamin Lee Whorf put it in this way: "Actually, thinking is most mysterious, and by far the greatest light upon it that we have is thrown by the study of language. This study shows that the forms of a person's thoughts are controlled by inexorable laws of pattern of which he is unconscious. These patterns are the unperceived intricate systematizations of his own language — shown readily enough by a candid comparison and contrast with other languages, especially those of a different linguistic family. His thinking itself is in a language — in English, in Sanskrit, in Chinese. And every language is a vast pattern-system, different from others, in which are culturally ordained the forms and categories by which the personality not only communicates, but also analyzes nature, notices or neglects types of relationships and phenomena, channels his reasoning, and builds the house of his consciousness."* Because this regularity exists in the structure of symbolic systems, the conceptions represented by symbols are not only free from the immediacy of the given situation, but they are capable of organizing a relatively stable world out of the fleeting manifold of sense impressions. Through them, we transform the unstable contents of direct experience into stable conceptions of objects with relatively enduring meaning and with continuing relationships to each other. The evaluative rules that structure symbolic systems contribute to their stability and to their ability to incorporate new meanings into the established system. They are thus the most important basis for the way in which human society organizes itself and its knowledge of the world. The very conception of the "world" as a stable entity is only possible because of the existence of symbols. By the same token, the "real worlds" created by human cultures for the persons operating within them are inescapably dependent upon the structure of their symbolic systems. This type of evaluation, because it is dependent on symbolic rules of right and wrong, defines obligations.

Where symbols, for instance language, are socially shared and their meanings standardized to a high degree, they become the prime vehicles of communication. Symbolic communication is thus constrained by two factors: the physical-social

*Language, Thought, and Reality, Selected Writings of Benjamin Lee Whorf, edited by John B. Carroll, The MIT Press, 1956, p. 252.

arrangements of communication channels, and the nature of the symbolisms that permit communication of certain types of experiences.

Symbolic systems, that is, the possible arrangements of symbolic patterns, as they are given by a language, then have three socially significant dimensions which we encountered in the epistemological analysis of symbolic mapping: the communicative dimension, the internal structure of the symbolic system itself, and the relationship between the particular symbol and its experiential referents. All three aspects or dimensions of symbolism are of importance in our context. It seems that the communicative dimension of symbolism does affect its internal structure as Hegel, and after him George Herbert Mead have endeavored to show. In discussing the dialectic method Hegel claims that it represents the most adequate tool for the analysis of thought and society, because it captures both the dynamic tension in the social process and in the movement of ideas.

As an illustration of this point, let us paraphrase Hegel's treatment of "love": The first "moment" in love is that I do not wish to be an independent person for myself, in that if I were only that I would feel incomplete and faulty. The second moment is that I gain myself in another person, that I reach my worth in that other person, and the other reaches his worth in me. Love is therefore a great contradiction which rationality fails to understand, since there is nothing harder to grasp than the assertion and denial of independence in self-consciousness, which love supersedes, but also retains. Love is the production and the solution of this contradiction simultaneously. In its resolution it produces moral unity.

Hegel expresses the view that "moral unity," or as we would put it, a socially binding evaluative standard, arises in the reflexive social relationship through the loyal commitment of one person to another in which the first person "gains himself," including knowledge of himself, through the eyes of the other. One could say that it is this reflexive relationship of "role taking" that produces the synthesis "moral unity," and thus society. The communicative nature of the reflexive relationship is supposedly expressed in the structure of Hegel's particular symbolism, the dialectic.

The postulated relationship between the structure of symbolic systems and the fundamental communicative processes becomes much clearer in the statement of George Herbert Mead. He tries to formulate a theory that derives the nature and structure of symbolism from the nature and structure of the interactive process. Interaction and communication among organisms may simply proceed through gestures. "Gestures" Mead defines as incipient acts; they are not necessarily symbols.* A gesture is simply the visible part of the total act, a sign of the total act that must be interpreted since the total act itself is of significance to the other organism, not merely the gesture. As long, however, as communication proceeds only through gestures, or the reading of immediately visible signs, the orientation of the communicating organisms is restricted to the presently given; both anticipation and recall are very limited in their temporal scope.

Certain gestures, however, sound gestures or vocal gestures, may affect the organism that perceives them in the same way in which they affect the organism producing them. They therefore become potential material for symbols, since they have, so to speak, a physical existence apart from the communicating organisms. A sound, once made, cannot be called back. It is, in a sense, an object in itself to which a meaning becomes affixed that both organisms share. This is possible because in the interaction process an organism learns to react to his own responses as others react to them. He learns to anticipate the reactions of others. That means he adopts the perspective of the other, takes his role. He thus begins to view himself as an object, while at the same time he remains a subject. This is what appeared to Hegel such a complex contradiction: reflexivity.

The person remains a subject while he knows of himself only as an object. As soon as he reflects upon himself, the "I" becomes the "Me." But, while he is reflecting, there is still something, somebody who does the reflecting, to whom the reflection is related. This point of reference in subjective experience Mead also calls the "I." "I" and "Me," following Hegel's dialectic relationship (if we are not too literal with the termin-

*George Herbert Mead, *Mind, Self, and Society*, Chicago, University of Chicago Press, 1934.

ology), in their tension constitute the dynamic structure of the "Self."

Hegel and Mead have clarified an important point for us: reflexivity, selfhood, is a product of both interaction and symbolism. It is possible because symbolism creates a characteristic distance between the directly experienced real thing and the reference point of subjective experience, the subject or "I" in a triadic relationship of which the social partner, the "Thou" or other is a significant component. Again we encounter the point: Symbolization forces us to distinguish between subject and object. The symbol itself is something that we can point at as in Mead's vocal gesture; it is no longer an integral part of the organism itself. The symbol, in turn, points at a realm of intended meanings. Thus, symbolization creates the fixed stability of an organized world in essential opposition to the subject. Reflexivity is the necessary product in its differentiation between the experiencer and the experienced.

Reflexivity, then, is the focal point of the relationship between communication and social interaction and the structure of symbolism itself. It breaks the immediacy of the link between organism and environment. The subject is set free from the pressures of the presently given, and can transcend it through intentional planning; but in the process he now inescapably becomes the focus of his own reflection. The human agent emerges as a complex of activity and observation, incorporating the dynamic tension between subject and object in the almost constant process of reflexivity.

From this argument derives a further point: the reflecting self necessarily constructs a retroactive image of himself (George Herbert Mead's "Me"), as he, the subject, reflects upon his activities. Herein lies one reason why the maintenance of a continuing identity of the self is one of the most powerful organizing principles of action. Reflexive selfhood forces the constant placement of experienced meanings, including those felt to be attributes of the self, into the context of symbolic systems and their evaluative standards. The trend toward consistency and continuity implied in the concept "identity" follows, in part, from this. It is linked with powerful motivational forces.

At the same time interaction, which is necessarily reflexive, in requiring that the "I" view itself in the perspective of the other as an object, the "Me," implies a constant shifting of perspectives. This is Mead's "learning through taking the role of the other," through which a potentially considerable repertory of social perspectives is acquired. Thus, it is not only true that I learn to see myself as an object and construct a continuing identity of myself over time, but also that I learn to see myself as an object from different points of view, and in terms of different evaluative standards. Almost paradoxically we can say that the emergence of identity of the self and the learning of diverse roles are two aspects of the same process.

To recapitulate: symbols are treated as fixed means of representing conceptions of intended objects. They are interrelated in symbolic systems which are structured by binding and necessarily evaluative rules; they make possible the construction of a stable world. At the same time symbols and symbolic systems are linked in the most intimate way with the structure of the interactive process, a relationship expressed in the phenomenon of reflexivity and selfhood. The stabilization of the self in the process of identity formation, then, is one necessary component in the total process of symbolic representation and construction of the world.

Chapter III

Orientation Systems and Reality Tests

The Coordination of Space and Time Orientation

The world of object concepts and the symbolic system in terms of which it is defined structure, among other things, the context of time and space into which the objects and the subject are placed, beyond the most rudimentary time-space extension. The framework of space, corresponding to the emergence of object concepts, develops through several stages of socialization, forming one important, basic aspect of the structure of the cognitive field. The progression begins with the disjointed sensory spaces in the context of which action schemata may emerge, unifying them in turn. Each sensory space originally has its own system of "coordinates" for the placement of experiences. There develops gradually a more or less integrated framework of experienced, or social space — without entirely superseding even in the adult the primitive forms.

The foundations are built in the repeated experience of effort in the manipulation of spatially distributed things. The child begins to note the spatial relations which unite perceived objects to each other, at first in a "topological" way. "This primitive, topological space is purely internal to the particular figure whose intrinsic properties it expresses, as opposed to spatial relationships of the kind which enable it to be related to other figures. Thus it has none of the features possessed by a space capable of embracing all possible figures, and the only relation between two or more figures comprehended by topological operations is that of simple one-one and bi-continuous correspondence, the basis of "homeomorphism" or structural equivalence between figures. With projective and Euclidian space we encounter a new and different problem, that of locating objects and their configurations relative to one another, in accordance with general perspective or projective systems, or according to co-ordinate axes. Projective or Euclidian structures are therefore more complex in organization and are only evolved at a later stage in the child's development."*

Piaget sketches here different modes of orientation to space. The transition from the simple orientation system of topological space to the more complex ones of the later ages also requires the coordination of the child's viewpoint with those of others. "The child's own point of view, which is the source of simple perspective, can give rise to a genuine representation, one that anticipates and reconstructs as well as records, only in so far as it is distinguished from other viewpoints; and this process can only occur within the framework of a global coordination. The child can only discover his own viewpoint as he becomes able to envisage those of other observers."** Distances are not measured, in childhood, by referring them to an abstract set of measurements, which are quite meaningless to a child, but in terms of concrete experiences: energy is required to get "there" from "here." Most of the significant distance experiences are social in nature; the character of social interaction itself requires spatial coordination through the coordination of efforts. The sharedness of such experiences establishes socially significant landmarks. One moves from one socially placed landmark to another, through certain experiences of common significance, and the residue of these activities constitutes, then, the framework of experienced space in which a child lives. For the early school child, the landmarks of the home, the school, certain stores, form orienting devices on his "map" of the environment.

The child's "map" of his environment is definitely distorted if compared to the structure of physical space. It is built up within the system for spatial operations which he has developed, and it is structured by outstanding marks which receive their importance through the experiences associated with them, usually experiences which are socially regularized. This remains true, to a somewhat lesser extent, even for the adult. His perception of space is also distorted, if compared to the scientifically represented space. For example, social distance between classes, transportation difficulties and the like may lead a person to

*Jean Piaget and Barbel Inhelder, *The Child's Conception of Space*, translated by F. J. Langdon and J. L. Lunzer, Routledge and Kegan Paul, London, 1956, p. 153.
**Piaget and Inhelder, op cit., p. 243.

imagine a neighborhood far away which is actually close by. Nevertheless, this "crooked" experiential space defines the spatial context in which persons live. In childhood the "distortions" are especially notable, because of the more primitive and self-centered system of spatial operations of which children are capable, and because of their limited spatial experience. But even in adult persons, it requires effort to overcome the distortions of the "mental map" of the environment in terms of which practical spatial orientation occurs.

The development of the sense of time goes through analogous stages, from the very early awareness of tim locations that are "different from now," where past and future are simply grouped together in one "non-present," to the clear differentiation of a time series. At the early stages time seems to consist of "immediacy" and "non-immediacy." Through the gradual emergence of an extension of his experiences over time, the child orients himself again in terms of socially significant landmarks. The social orientation to, measuring of, and the regulation of activities in time is an important basis of social coordination. The degree to which social coordination requires shared orientation systems in time and space for certain domains of activity is frequently overlooked.

Wilbert E. Moore points out that much social behavior is ordered and regulated by common definitions, assumptions, and actions with regard to the location of events in time. "Certain activities, for example, require simultaneous actions by a number of persons, or at least their presence at a particular time — the starting of a work shift at a factory, the departure of a fishing boat from a wharf or beach, or the calling of an association meeting to order. Thus one element of temporal ordering is synchronization. Other activities require that actions follow one another in a prescribed order; thus sequence is part of the temporal order. For still other activities the frequency of events during a period of time is critical; thus rate also is one of the ways that time impinges on social behavior. For all these elements of social coordination the term timing is useful, since it denotes precisely the critical importance of some temporal order, while leaving open the kind of requirement or the rigidity with which the activity in question is to be related to time as an inexorable variable."*

*Wilbert E. Moore, *Man, Time, and Society,* John Wiley, New York and London, 1963.

The socially essential coordination of individual orientation in time and space is built upon the shared aspects of spatial and temporal "maps" which persons develop. It consists of the establishment of spatial and temporal landmarks and domains of meaning which structure the practical world of the "natural attitude" in similar ways in the participants of a group.

The Collective and Individual Contexts of Interpretation

We must go beyond elementary time-space orientation. As we learned from William James, domains of reality which are meaningfully apprehended by the person are structed around his vital concerns. In order to discover the principle of structure in the interpretation of experience, we must grasp the ordering of these vital concerns. Normally, they are organized in the patterns of a person's typical social activities. It is in this context that his cognitive field is structured. Shared activities, which are scheduled and placed, we find, form the basis of this structure. The origins of object meanings can be found in the activity patterns.

Symbolic representation, and the construction of generalized maps of reality, lift the orientation system beyond the immediately given pattern of activity. Instead of being bound to the concrete arrangements of which he is a part, the person can and does orient himself in terms of symbolically defined type constructs of reality. There arise symbolically structured domains of meaning which remain, however, structured around the basic functional concerns of the individual personality and his social participations. We may say that the cognitive field of the individual is structured in terms of the differentiated personal, collective, and institutional concerns in which he is involved.

Inasmuch as these concerns are socially regularized, the person is likely to avail himself of the collectively sanctioned orientation systems provided by his social roles. Each experience is assigned its specific placement and interpretation by being "treated" in the typical frame of reference of a social role. It is thus assigned a collective significance and meaning, by being incorporated into the organization of realities relative to the structure of vital concerns in the *collectivity* or the institutional domain.

A second, analytically distinguished process of interpretation, centering around the vital concerns of the *person* as

such, focusing on his maintenance of personal identity, inter-
sects the first one. Each experience, we have said, is assigned
its social significance and meaning by being treated in terms
of a role specific frame of reference. The same experience is
also, inescapably, part of a person's individual history. It is
"his" experience and must be interpreted in relation to what
he believes himself to be. In the case of the person who plays
a social role with extreme "role distance," essentially as something "alien" to himself, the reality interpretation connected
with the role is assigned a subordinate significance. His identity is preserved in separation from the role. In other cases
there may be complete identification with the role, so that
both modes of interpretation merge.

The individual's conception of himself, his identity, was
found to be dynamically related to his understanding of the
world. His conception of identity places him into the context of the world, in relation to significant other persons, and
in relation to groups with which he compares himself or from
which he differentiates himself. His identity is anchored in a
sense of placement and belonging; many of his roles demand by
contrast a primacy of impersonal achievement and performance.
The standards which guide the interpretation of experiences
in these two contexts are, therefore, not necessarily the same.

The conception of identity must be maintained in sometimes
rapidly changing action contexts. It is the result of stabilization rather than of unmoving stability. Identity maintenance,
thus, requires the constant re-interpretation of the past and
of the future in the light of the present concerns. The organization of the cognitive field, then, emerges as a process of
constant structuring and ordering, or interpretation. It is guided
by the repertory of role-specific frames of reference offered to
a person by his social participations, and by the inherent organization of these frames of reference into major institutional
and cultural domains. It is unified, however, for the person by
his constant interpretation of his past and future in the light
of his present conception of his identity.

The same could be said of groups. The maintenance of a
continuing group identity requires its continuous reconstruction. It has often been observed that the writing of collective
histories may serve this purpose, being an attempt to project
present values and norms into the past. The reinterpretation

of past and future is one of the most important mechanisms in the stabilization of the present conception of the group's reality. Changes in the history textbooks under the press of political changes in the present may illustrate this point.

In this section we have sketched the dynamics of the interpretation of experience in the context of a structured cognitive field. We found these dynamics grounded in the spaced and timed pattern of activities of people, but transcending the immediacy of these patterns through the processes of symbolic representation and transformation. The most prominent orienting devices remain the symbolically defined frames of reference of social roles, which are integrated by the constant process of the individual's or the group's construction of his own identity in the context of the world as he or they know it.

Frames of Reference and Theories

We have explored the broad outlines and the significance of the processes of reality interpretation. The term interpretation is deliberately diffuse. An experience is interpreted by being placed into a context; here interpretation provides the orientational function of placement of events in relation to each other. We may also speak of interpretation when we mean "explanation," the derivation of a specific statement about an event from a system of general ones, or within a formal pattern of statements. Our further progress now requires somewhat more specific analyses of the processes of interpretation, involving frames of reference, theories, explanation, and reality tests.

Before we turn to this task, a general caution must be observed. Actual experience of reality and orientations to reality are interrelated in a complex way. We described certain contexts or extensions of actuality which are so general that all specific orientations or frames of reference operate within them. In this sense the actuality precedes a person's specific orientation to it. The experience may force changes in orientation. Yet, in another sense, orientations precede experience in that they define what a person "looks for." The broad direction of his reality search, and his sensitization to experience are provided by his "values." Such value attitudes define his "outlook," establish some of the relations among objects, and between objects and the person himself. These broad values, which account for the general approach to reality, and the style of responses to new situations, are at a more specific level expressed in metaphysics and epistemologies. There are two sides to these broad orientations: the side of substantive images (metaphysics and theories) and the side of active procedures (epistemologies and methods). The interplay among actual experience, metaphysics and epistemologies in the process of its interpretation may be implicit, but it is always inescapable. This interplay is an essentially creative procss; in the following attempt to distinguish certain aspects which are important for our context there is no pretension of completeness.

Modes of reality construction and their more specific components are best described by analyzing "theories" which are both attempts at summarizing sets of reality constructs, and rationales for their explanation. One may think of the theories of science in this connection; but by no means all theories are scientific. There are magical and religious theories, to mention only two which fall outside the realm of empirical science. All such theories, however, share an essential structure and have some equivalent components. Theories are themselves embedded in a context, as they provide the interpretive context for specific experiences.

Theories, that is systematic statements summarizing and interpreting some aspect of experienced reality, can be analyzed into a set of functional components, including the orientational, the descriptive or organizing, and the explanatory function. They are set into the contexts of epistemological and metaphysical decisions on one hand, and methodological procedures and modes of reality tests on the other. This analysis will yield insights into the nature of orientation systems in general, since all persons, not just scientists, hold and apply theories of some kind. The resulting insights can also be applied to the study of the purely social organization of reality constructs which is found in social roles.

All societies offer frameworks for the "normal" perception and interpretation of reality by institutionalizing broad frames of reference which define the ways in which experiences should be approached and understood. This fact itself has been mentioned; we now can spell out in more detail what a "frame of reference" is. The matter will be best clarified by referring to symbolic constructions which are beyond doubt intended to state a "reality," namely philosophical and scientific theories and their frames of reference. For illustrative purposes, we will refer primarily to social scientific theories which presumably state our working knowledge of society. The analytic concepts gained are, however, not restricted to these theories.

Theories, quite generally, fulfill three functions: they specify a particular orientation to the subject matter; they provide categories for the description and classification of observations; and they offer communicable explanations of the relevant experienced events. In this sense any reality experience to which a definite meaning is assigned is embedded in the context of a theory, which specifies its value extension, its symbolic extension, and relates it to the communication extension by means of a general orientation, a categorical scheme, and a type of explanation. Even the incomplete theory thus constitutes a specific "map" of some aspect of reality. Its necessity for any knowledge was shown before.

The first two functions of a theory, which are to provide a general orientation and a categorical scheme, may be grouped together under the name "frame of reference." On one side, a frame of reference must be anchored in an epistemological position and is thus related to the larger context of the theory which defines implicitly or explicitly its relevant criteria of "truth." On the other side, the frame of reference must be relevant to the way in which specific experiences are recorded and classified. It is thus connected to a methodology.

In the realm of social theories it is easy to find illustrations of the significance of epistemologies and categorical schemes which underlie specific theories. The reader may think, for example, of the differences in theoretical positions between Emile Durkheim and George Simmel. Each man's position implies a fairly definite, if not necessarily clearly stated epistemology, orientation, and categorical scheme. Durkheim decides to study "social facts" which he sees in analogy to "things." They are exterior to the individual, just like natural facts or physical things, and they are constraining for the individual in the sense that they are "hard" facts, which the individual simply cannot ignore with impunity. By elimination the domain of social facts is that which is not part of the realm of nature as such, nor purely an attribute of the individual. Social facts belong to the external world, and they constitute a set of conditions to which the individual must adapt himself. The study of social facts,

then, properly concentrates on the attributes of groups or collectivities, such as suicide rates and the like.

For Simmel, on the other hand, all knowledge is relative to
the needs of life itself. Truth is determined by the needs of
human nature, and the reality which is apprehended as well.
Philosophical systems, for instance, are "true" if their picture
of the world presents a meaningful whole and permits us to
fit the known segments into it. Science is for him not the only
way of forming the world. Art, religion, metaphysics, and other
systems are independent ways of understanding. The final unity
of the different fields of mental activity rests in the unity of
human life itself. In this mode of thinking it is natural for
Simmel to resolve the collectivity or superindividuality into
reciprocity. He sees society as an emergent phenomenon, resulting from the interactions of living individuals.

Durkheim's concentration on what he considers "social facts"
gives his work a pervasively different slant from Simmel's work
because Simmel's concentration on the realm of lived meanings and the study of "social forms" relates to an entirely different conception of factual datum. We do not mean,
incidentally, that epistemologies necessarily determine theories.
We do mean that the two are necessarily related. An epistemology answers questions such as these: "What constitutes 'truth'
in the first place?" "What kind of knowledge, obtained under
what conditions, and by whom, may be accepted as valid?"

Epistemological decisions thus dictate broad preferences for
the kinds of experiential bases on which knowledge is to be
constructed. One could say that the epistemological position
sensitizes the observer to certain aspects of encountered realities
and desensitizes him to others. The history of philosophy and
of religion shows the vast range of epistemological positions and
corresponding metaphysics. But the manifold is not infinite.
Philosophers like Dilthey, Rothacker, Jaspers, Pepper have attempted to sort out the fundamental possibilities with considerable convergence in their results. The epistemologies arising
from the socio-cultural experience of man thus far are limited
in their range. Important for us is the fact that epistemologies
and metaphysical systems that underlie any specific theories
form internally consistent configurations of cognitive styles and
that they define preferences for certain kinds of encountered
experiences over others.

Stephen C. Pepper sets forth an analysis of what he calls "word hypotheses," that is, fundamental images of the world which correspond to metaphysical systems. Each system is related to certain views of evidence and corroboration. Pepper distinguished four broad types: formism, based on the "root metaphor" of similarity and exemplified by the philosophy of Platonic idealism, uses as a criterion of truth the degree of similarity which a description has to its object of reference. Mechanism, using as its root metaphor and machine, is illustrated by the philosophy of Hobbes. It considers truth to arise out of causation (stimulation) and adjustment of the organism. Contextualism, using as its root metaphor the historic event, views truth in the pragmatic and operational context of action. It is associated with the work of such philosophers as James, Mead and others. Finally, in the case of organicism, the basic root metaphor is that of the integrated organism; its truth theory emphasizes the notion of coherence. It is typically associated with the "objective idealism" of Hegel and similar thinkers.

Pepper's work, while to be taken as illustrative only, makes the point very well that epistemologies are tied to metaphysics, and that they have a broad, sensitizing function. We can think of it in analogy to the first phase of the perceptual process as the psychologist describes it. It corresponds to the broad expectation of certain kinds of experiences.

A second aspect of the orientational function of theories consists of the basic model of the reality to be represented. Pepper tends to give these basic models which he calls "root metaphors" priority over almost everything else. They provide, in his view, the encompassing images of reality itself. Be this as it may, in the case of social theories the significance of basic models of society, for example as an organism, as a machine, as a pattern of historical events, and others can be easily shown. Like epistemology, such basic models, or root metaphors, rest on pre-empirical, metaphysical commitments. Together with the epistemology, they define certain aspects of the reality under study as important or unimportant, as accessible to the observer or inaccessible. Both of these facets may enter into what we should call the "preference system" of the observer: the more or less systematic tendency of the observer to select certain experiences as relevant and to dismiss others as irrelevant. Such

preferences are a more specific matter than the general sensitization of the observer mentioned above. They correspond roughly
to the second and third phase in the perceptual process which
we discussed before.

As an illustration of preference systems we may again refer
to Durkheim and Simmel respectively. Durkheim, proceeding
in terms of a quasi-organismic model of the social system and
a positivist epistemology, concerned himself with groups as
groups; Simmel, viewing society in terms of an individualistic-
interaction model and a quasi-Kantian epistemology studied
the activities of individuals and how they impinge upon each
other in the generation of "social forms." Both men clearly
preferred different aspects of social reality for their investigation and treatment. Their theories show that epistemology and
basic model of reality together enter into the determination of
the observer's preference system, and that preference systems
both limit and sharpen the perspective of the observer by bring-
ing out those aspects which he selects as significant.

The general orientation and its preference system, which
constitute the first component of a theory, must be connected
with a scheme for the description of what is apprehended. Such
a scheme provides related categories for the description and
the recording of what has been observed. The categorical scheme,
then, is the second functional component of the theory. It permits the reporting and arrangement of information in terms
of units which have significance both for the epistemological
and metaphysical bases of the system and for the
explanatory statements which are finally produced. The categorical scheme as such is a static set of concepts. The operation
of recording information and the task of providing explanations
must be guided by rules which are used more or less consist-
ently over time. These rules for the application of the categorical scheme to the data of experience, are an aspect of
"methodologies."

Again, we must point out that every theory, and not only
scientific ones, require methodologies. Experiences, once recorded, must be connected with descriptive and explanatory
generalizations. Certain symbolic transformations must follow
more or less stable rules. The methodology provides these rules
and the rationale for them.

The final functional aspect of a theory is provided by the

explanatory system itself. Often only such systems are specifically called theories; this practice is useful only where the frames of reference consisting of epistemologies, preference systems, categorical schemes and the methodologies to which they are connected, are highly standardized. The kinds of explanation provided by a theory differ depending on its ultimate purpose. Ernest Nagel attempted to reduce the manifold of explanations to a typology of four kinds of explanations used in scientific contexts, the deductive, probabilistic, functional, and genetic types. The variety of actually used explanations is undoubtedly far wider, especially outside the domain of science itself. One may think of magical or mystical explanations; they do qualify by our usage for the term "theory." At any rate, the inherent model of explanation will depend on the nature of the problem dealt with by the theory, and also upon the epistemology and the frame of reference. The mode of explanation defines the central, logical structure of the theory itself. It is a formal way of relating the explanendum to firmly established reality constructs. Substantively, the theory is expressed in statements of varying generality, from which it is possible to derive specific explanations concerning experienced events.

Theories, the Experience of Certainty, and Reality Tests

Theoretically provided explanations are always potentially subject to test. In the domain of scientific theories, these tests consist essentially in the verification of conditional predictions derived from the theory; that is "if and when" certain conditions are present which, according to the theory should give rise to a particular type of event, then it should be possible to observe the event. If the event does not occur, the theory has dubious validity. Even in science, however, not all tests are of this specific variety; they may be concerned, for example with the parsimony of the explanation — with preference given to the most parsimonious. Since in our present discussion the intention is to illuminate the general organization of theories, and not only of scientific ones, it is necessary for us to consider the larger variety of tests which are actually applied to theories by social agents. There are many non-empirical, and even non-logical tests applied by the users of a theory. Explanations, then, are accepted or rejected as appropriate or inappropriate

depending on their fit with such tests. In every case, the test of
a theory must relate the explanatory statement in a convincing
way to a source of unquestionable reality. Only by establishing such relationship to a basis in certainty can explanations be
accepted as plausible.

We must turn to a phenomenological investigation of the
sources of certainty in human experience in order to understand the variety of reality tests applied in society. There is a
socially shared experience in which the paramount reality of
the manipulable thing is constantly tested; this is the experience of "work." The analysis of work and of its social organization yields insights into one of the two most important connections between the forming and elaboration of reality constructs, and the structure of society, since work represents the
most important base of contact with the reality of "hard facts."

What is work? It can be best illustrated by contrasting it
with "play."* In work one confronts a set of objects relevant
to a task which requires that the objects or their relationship be
changed in some way. The change accomplished is irrevocable
by wish or pretense; to be undone, further work is required.
Work consumes energy; its results cannot be simply taken back,
in the way in which one can take back an erroneous thought.
This irrevocability of work requires, then, the serious commitment of the worker to one central perspective relative to the
objects with which he is working. This commitment to the
thing before him is a necessary requirement for his "attending"
to his work properly. We are not implying that work always
is done enthusiastically or lovingly. But even the "alienated"
worker must, while at work, attend to the thing at hand, in
the light of the requirements of the task. Even his resentment
of the work assignment does not alter the fact that while he is
actually working at anything other than a completely routinized task which can be accomplished virtually in the unconscious
manner of a sleep walker (and there are few work tasks that
routine), he must attend with serious commitment to one proper
perspective to the realities which he is handling.

Giving the term "working" a somewhat special meaning, Alfred Schutz writes: "Working, then, is action in the outer world,
based upon a project and characterized by the intention to bring

*Again, my indebtedness to the work of Alfred Schutz must be men-
tioned. See Alfred Schutz, op. cit.

about the projected state of affairs by bodily movements. Among all the described forms of spontaneity that of working is the most important one for the constitution of the reality of the world of daily life. . . . The wide-awake self integrates in its working and by its working its present, past and future into a specific dimension of time; it realizes itself as a totality in its working acts; it communicates with Others through working acts; it organizes the different spatial perspectives of the world of daily life through working acts."*

In "play," on the other hand, the player is allowed and even encouraged to adopt alternative perspectives. He is expected to have a detached attitude to the play, at least after it is concluded; this holds true even in the instance of competitive play. But particularly appropriate is the example of a child's role playing, "play acting." The child adopts and discards different roles (and the corresponding perspectives) without any irrevocable commitment. Play, then, is revocable and forms a contrast with the serious singlemindedness of work; if in work the concern with reality is supreme, in play it is subordinated to the fun of sheer symbolization.

To be sure, what is one man's work may be another man's play by this definition. But societies quite in general are reasonably consistent in their definition of work roles. They are those roles that require the serious dedication to one central perspective toward the object, which must be changed in some way: there must be an output. Everything related to work somehow "matters" very much; the requisites of play may be more dear to our hearts, more enjoyable than the tools of work, but they "matter" less. An activity that allows a change of perspective in terms of "it does not really matter" thus is play: work does not permit such withdrawal into a different perspective.

Play is, of course, of great significance in socialization, in establishing an extensive repertory of symbolic possibilities, and expressive activity. Playfulness makes possible the manifold of different perspectives, among which we can shift almost at will. But it is work that forces us into the commitment to the "vivid presence" so that only one of the symbolic possibilities, only one of the value alternatives, and only the seriously rele-

*Alfred Schutz, Collected Papers, Vol. I, *The Problem of Social Reality*, Martinus Nijhoff, The Hague, 1962.

vant communicative channels are considered. The experience of
the "hard reality" requires as a necessary prerequisite the hard
attitude, the serious, irrevocable dedication of the worker at
work. This may be further illustrated by the fact that the concepts "work" and "reality" alike connote an experiential complex of seriousness, of discipline, and of dedication, even of
compulsion. Such are the attributes of the orientation to work;
they are clear in the expected orientation built into the work
roles we know. Although we may resent such demands, reject
them, feel constrained and alienated in such roles, this does
not alter the structure of the work orientation itself.

The very broad orientation to reality implied in work restricts
the types of value contexts with which it is compatible. This
orientation can be characterized as that of "comprehensive values."* It constitutes an openness for the requirements of a
situation, whatever it may be, and an acceptance of general
rules and techniques which are applied to assure mastery over
the encountered world. An orientation in terms of comprehensive values is non-restrictive in the sense that it does not
permit the elimination of situational questions or problems
on the grounds of "propriety" or pre-established beliefs of a
substantive nature. The orientation is fundamentally anchored
in the experience of mastery and technical power. This comprehensive value orientation is rarely, if ever, found without
being limited in the range of its application by other values.
It is dominant, generally speaking, in the domain of autonomous work. The basis of certainty deriving from the experience
of things in the framework of work is one important source
of reality tests, especially since work roles also structure simultaneously social and individual concerns. We will have to
concern ourselves with modes of reality construction and with
reality tests in the world of work.

By contrast the reality and certainty of the interpretive order
or of "beliefs" constitutes a different phenomenological variety
from the reality of the "thing" and the latter's social and experiential base in the realm of work. It directs us to the second most important relation between reality constructs and the
social structure; the interpretive order includes all reality constructs used in the legitimation and condemnation of activity;
it thus embraces a wide range of beliefs, religious, moral, ideo-

*This term is freely adapted from the usage given by Otto von Mering,
A Grammar of Human Values, University of Pittsburgh Press.

logical and other. An interpretive order as such is never experienced in direct actuality. It assigns meanings and context to actually encountered things, but it is only directly actualized in the rare case of the genuine mystic.

The legitimation of an act presupposes cognitive constructions of the self, of the group, and even of the encompassing universe, which permit the finding of good reasons why the particular action should or should not be legitimate. These cognitive constructions are, of course, "world views." In another terminology, they are value systems in the sense that they are structured as sources of legitimacy for action.

The ultimate experiential base of such value systems lies in the felt confrontation with the sacred or holy which inspires awe and is seen as the final source of both the individual's and the group's worth. More concretely, the value system relates to the experience of social boundaries; the feeling of legitimacy and righteousness is grounded in the experience of acceptance and belonging, of protection by the warmth of a worthy group. Both "external" boundaries, which delimit the group from the outside social world, and "internal" boundaries which delimit the bounds of good membership are felt in this way.

The external boundary is most clearly recognized when it is threatened by an alien and hostile group. The internal boundary, which is defined by rules of right and wrong, is most clearly recognized when deviants provoke a feeling of indignation and heroes create a sense of pride and honor.

Legitimating value systems are always, in the last analysis, tied to such experienced social boundaries. They are "isolative"* in the sense that they may rule out issues and problem situations as improper and even define them as unreal. Within their boundaries, isolative value systems may encompass and tolerate comprehensive values even though comprehensive values are not grounded on social boundaries. In every case, however, isolative values define the domain within which variant values may operate.

The interpretive order, which results from the combined value systems, is clearly structured into different levels of generality and different problems of social action. At the most general level we would find the ultimate values which are seen as sources of legitimacy and worth and do not require further

*Another term borrowed freely from Otto von Mering, op. cit.

justification. these values provide the broad rationales for the more specific levels of legitimation or "proximate values" which have direct linkage with the routines of daily life.

Intersecting these levels, the number and differentiation of which can be shown to vary with the degree of social differentiation, one may distinguish several domains which reflect the major institutional spheres of social activity, such as religion, government, commerce and other spheres. Clearly, the differentiation of an interpretive order reflects the differentiation of society itself. Values which may be distinct in the highly differentiated society of modern industrialism may be completely or partially fused in social systems of lesser complexity.

Such a system of legitimating beliefs or values shapes the way in which a subject interprets the experiences and the social regularities which he finds. The experienced reality of this system stems primarily from the vital concern for consistency and worthwhileness which is adduced in the act of legitimation. The emerging order of reality is, however, rarely simply and unproblematically given, especially where the experience of social boundaries is intense. It is a "posited" reality which is not merely existing, but which "must exist." If it is successfully threatened, there may appear a reality shock in which the subject may feel: "If this is not true, one cannot believe anything any more . . . "

Value systems thus need to be defended at least if there are alternative values on the horizon or if other challenges exist. While value systems are used in the legitimation of significant acts, they themselves are often defensively asserted. This, together with the fact that their acceptance rests on the identification of the individual with bounded groups, points again to the linkage between values and social authority.

If the social organization of work must be studied to understand the sociology of reality constructs, it is also necessary to study the social organization of authority to understand the sociology of legitimating beliefs. An individual's relation to authority and the specific social boundaries and substantive values which it may represent, however, is a complex matter because the acceptance or rejection of constituted authority is an expression of the individual's identifications. The dynamics of alienation and loyal commitment must be examined in order to understand the dynamics of belief systems.

Phenomenological reflection leads to the recognition of the centrality of social authority for both the structure and the dynamics of belief systems and the interpretive orders to which they give rise. A large number of social science investigations support this point and converge with the phenomenological result. Max Weber, in his analysis of legitimate authority, showed the intimate connection between the structure of authority systems and the values legitimating them. The study of the "authoritarian personality" showed, from a completely different perspective, how an individual's mode of identity construction (using my terminology) and self-legitimation relates to his attitude toward constituted authority and established group boundaries. The cognitive styles of the "open" and the "closed" mind (Rokeach) describe essentially ways in which an individual interprets concrete situations and brings his beliefs into play. They, too, are reflections of the underlying modes of identity formation and the types of social commitments. The reality tests of the interpretive order relate to the certainties arising from the individual's concern with his identity and his commitment or subjection to a socially constituted authority system.

We can, then, describe a set of reality tests which correspond to different modes of constructing reality, and which are socially assigned to different types of orientations and situations. Where work is predominant, the reality test consists normally in the pragmatic establishment of workability. This test may be entirely "pragmatic-empirical," or it may be connected with various theoretical contexts. The stronger the additional criterion of symbolic, theoretical consistency of the assertion to be tested within itself and with other assertions is considered, the more will the test approach the "deductive" variety. Where the dynamics of a person's interpretive order are involved, the reality test is likely to be the relationship between the assertion to be tested and the legitimations of established authority. This can work in both the positive or negative way: there is the "authoritative" test — simply accepting the assertions of authority as true, and the "alienative" test — the belief that the assertions of the rejected authority must necessarily be false. Where the individual's experience of his personal identity is directly invoked, we may speak of the "mystical" tests — the test based upon the certainty of an individual's personal, strongly emotional insights or revelations.

Reality tests, we saw, link symbolized experiences and theories to the sources of subjective certainty. These sources of subjective certainty, however, were found to consist of socially structured commitments, especially to the world of work, and to the loyalties and authorities, to the legitimating claims of groups. They are connected to the variety of modes of reality construction, which we did not attempt to reduce to a simplifying typology, but which we analyzed into their essential components.

The Structure of Cognitive Action and Its Social Organization

We have discussed the significance of the construction of symbolic maps for the existence of any knowledge. The anchorage of symbolization in the structure of perception and in the gradual construction of a stabilized world and corresponding self were analyzed in their interplay between experience in manipulation and reflective selfhood, and interpretive efforts to achieve meaningful unity of world and self. We recognized the strategic role which commitments and vital concerns of a person play in the structuring of his experience. Given such commitments and vital concerns, orientation systems arise which limit the choice of epistemologies, of preference systems, categorical schemes and explanatory theories as well as of reality tests.

The most important consideration is, however, that cognitive action is socially structured. It is shaped, of course, by the available symbolic systems, but also by the specific dynamics of the individual's participations in his social world. Work, and structured work roles emerged as one critical focus for the study of the social organization of cognitive actions; on the other side we concluded that the other critical focus is that of the link between the individual's identity and the authority system of his group (taken as the crucial symbolization of the legitimating beliefs which the group "stands for") — critical both in commitment and alienation.

Society defines the appropriateness of reality tests for many kinds of problems. The trained worker has been equipped with the necessary frame of reference and knowledge of appropriate tests to deal with the experiences of his work situations; the citizen, presumably, has acquired an understanding of the interpretive order of his group which gives him the proper orientation to collective challenges. Society can be seen as a vast distribution of different kinds of orientations (with frames of reference, and a repertory of theories linked to them) on one side, and a vast distribution of situations on the other. Normally, only the surgeon finds himself in the situation of performing an operation, or the teacher in the situation of teaching. It is in these matches of orientations and situations that socially recommended reality tests must prove their mettle, because here orientations must prove adequate to the management of concrete experiences and actions. The total distribution of orientations, and the allocation of situations to differently prepared people also has to meet a superordinate test: that of the workability of the whole society, in which, up to a degree, orientations and situations must match in order to permit the necessary coordination of social life itself.

Chapter IV

Networks of Cognitive Acts and Epistemic Communities

The Nature of the Interaction Process as Exchange and Socialization

We must now turn to the consideration of the interactive process itself. For the purposes at hand it is best to think of the prototype of interaction as reciprocal action: two agents who are aware of each other and pursue their own (rarely identical) objectives, and who face each other in an at least partly shared situation.

Each of the interacting agents is, of course, a conscious self. He does have a more or less stable and more or less elaborate conception of his own identity and of the situation in which he finds himself. He recognizes that the other participant also is a conscious self, thinks of himself in certain ways, and ascribes particular meanings to his situations. They communicate through shared symbols and ascribe to each other as well as to themselves relatively unified perspectives and, above all, intentions. Their views of the situation include each other and overlap at least in part.

Nevertheless, the situation is typically asymmetrical, in that the actions of each agent are guided by different intentions and somewhat different values, and therefore by different perspectives upon the situation. Upon their first meeting, and continuing in the course of the interaction, our two agents "size each other up." Each is trying to form, on the basis of whatever clues are presented to him, as accurate an image as he can of the other person, his background, his characteristics, and his likely intentions, which would include an assessment of how the other views him. Whether or not the thought occurs explicitly; in these aspects of an acquaintance each partner tries to figure out in what way the other might relate to his own plans and projects, and in what way he himself might be related to them. This does not have to be understood merely in the instrumental sense that people "use" each other (even though they often

60

do), but in the sense that they see the other's projects as impinging on their own.

We may think of the conversations and other relationships which may follow upon a first encounter of two agents as a series of exchanges. The agents each pursue somewhat different objectives, otherwise no exchange is possible. However, the pursuit of such different objectives will permit the participants either mutual gain, gain for one person, and loss for the other, or loss for both persons. If in the first stages the objectives of the exchange are likely to be informational on both sides, the purpose of the exchange, and maybe its very terms are likely to change rapidly as the action unfolds and as, to mention only one variable among the very many that might enter into the process, one agent establishes significant power over the other.

Each participant in the interaction situation acts on the basis of his hypothetical model of the other person, or, as Cooley puts it, on the basis of his image of the other. Simmel called attention to this tendency to create "types" for the persons we deal with in interaction. We thus orient ourselves to the other in terms of a type-like image of him. Such a type-like image will not only reflect the characteristics of the partner, but also features of the situational context, and it will be heavily influenced by the purposes and beliefs held by each agent.

Especially important in this type-like image of the other is the agent's construction of the other's objectives. He will probably try to affect the other's objectives in some way in order to assure his own "gain." He will try to manipulate the other's objectives, and will probably do so as long as he has objects under his control which the other person values. He thus exercises to some extent his power over the other person.

By exercising power and affecting his partner's objectives, he changes his action tendencies, and this means that he changes the characteristics of the other. The other also changes under indirect consequences of the interaction situation. He learns more about his partner, his motivations may change; in short, agents cannot be realistically treated as entirely stable units over time. Their specific action characteristics and dispositions will change as the situation changes. Interaction, then, involves a dynamic relationship among at least two, or more, changing elements. Actors try to direct the actual course of the other person's activity to mesh with their own projects, and they must necessarily admit to some changes on their own part. Interaction is, in part, a process of constant socialization.

It is difficult to overestimate the fluidity and the dynamic nature of interaction. The images of the partner, in terms of which an agent arranges his course of action, are very often built on subtle, and sometimes easily misread cues. Since this process is of great strategic value to each participant, each tries to control the presentation of such cues to the other. He will try to present a more or less stylized image of himself in line with his objectives, his identity, and his situational context. As Goffman puts it, he "presents himself" by managing the impression he creates. Such attempts at stylized self-interpretation undoubtedly aid in stabilizing the process of interaction in that they try to link the presently visible front which each agent presents to his partner with the imputation of an underlying and continuing identity.

The complexity of interaction relationships among changing agents is further increased by the fact that each must refer almost constantly to a variety of yardsticks of symbolic placement and evaluation as the nature of the immediate transactions change. The possibilities in varying interpretations of any single event are staggering, as we saw in the discussions above. Without counteracting trends, this would result in a breath-taking sequence of diverse social and personal images in the experience of interacting partners. The process is, however, stabilized by the attempt to maintain a continuing personal identity, and the ascription of lasting characteristics to others, and to limited activity systems, such as roles, organizations, and collectivities, in spite of real changes. Given the fact of change through interaction, which is inevitably at least a small change in the very attributes of the interacting persons, "identity" must almost constantly be reconstructed. All of us rewrite our personal histories after every major social experience. We check back, try to make sure that there is, after all, consistency and continuity. Where breaks in continuity occur, inconsistency must be admitted and the reasons have to be given. Personal histories, then, are often construed into periods and epochs, each with its own style, atmosphere and "contribution" to the continued, embracing growth of our self-understanding. For collectivities, such as nations or clubs, the same rules hold true and for the same reason. The writing of national histories, where it is not practiced for the sake of world-wide, disinterested scholarship, is usually nothing more nor less than the construction of national identities (including national "characters") after the fact. If members of the collectivity are to define a major aspect of their own, personal identity in collective terms, these attempts are of great social significance.

Interaction, then, involves in one very important aspect the transformation of each partner through socialization and the stabilization of the process through the construction and presentation of identities. Every interactive experience which an individual may have must thus become incorporated into two different contexts of meaning which are, as we saw in the discussion of interpretation, two different "histories" that intersect: (1) the order of the group and the meaning which the experience has in terms of its structural context, and (2) the order of personal identity and the significance and place the experience has in terms of the personal history. Every act may be interpreted and possibly legitimated in both of these two contexts: to the group and to the self.

Symbolic stabilization of the interaction process defines a network of activity systems, and identities which relate to the social activity systems, and domains of meaning. The stabilized and symbolically fixed interaction patterns must be coordinated with each other in experiential time and space. Here lies one basis of social coordination: in the agent there develops a specifically structured map of his social participations and their contexts, on which the significant activity systems and objects are placed in relation to each other and in relation to the self. Such a map has a distinct temporal and spatial base, in that the coordination of social arrangements is closely linked with the organization of time and space through visible landmarks and shared measures of the interstices.

The Cognitive Construction of Others and of Roles

The concrete point at which collective histories and personal identity intersect is that of the social role. Here we are dealing with relatively lasting, and sometimes highly segmental "preestablished" identities which are symbolically labeled in such a way that role-relevant situations, partners, and appropriate occupants are recognized as distinct. The image of the role develops into a cognitively coherent whole through the generalization of offered clues and by fitting it into the symbolically represented network of social coordination.

Each role is culturally characterized, as Siegfried Frederick Nadel showed, by a type construct which relates the role to a culturally elaborated system or network of roles. Nadel points out that role concepts are not inventions of social scientists, but are used by the people under study. They refer to expectations of behavior, and are, logically, both type and class concepts. They are usually more than mere class concepts which label a category of objects, in that role concepts refer to behavior, to interactive settings, and in that they establish patterns of normative conformities of purposive actions.*

We must add to this. The type construct of a role which is in actual social use, may encompass the normative models of the role, but deviates often from them. A type construct describes central tendencies found in a category of things; it accounts by means of a unified scheme for some aspect of the empirical variation found within this category. Role concepts are "types" in this sense.

The socially used type construct of a role specifies what characteristics the occupant of such and such a role usually would have. Its normative aspect states what characteristics he may, or should have, what orientations to the role-relevant situations he does or should develop, which appropriate theories and skills he should have or does have, and what the appropriate and the likely models of transactions among the role occupant and his partners are.

Role constructs are, thus, symbolic stabilizations of inherently changing and sometimes fleeting interactions. They are anchored in networks of symbolically defined relationships with other roles. They identify and at the same time define the perspectives, or orientations, which the role occupant is likely to have toward his partners, and the orientations which his partners are likely to have towards him. In their cognitive significance roles can be seen as the prime stabilizers of the orientational structure of society. They must be related to the encompassing conceptions of collective identities and must be compatible with the specific conceptions of personal identities held by their occupants.

At the same time, social roles designate a series of timed and

*Siefgried Frederick Nadel, *The Theory of Social Structure*.

spaced activities. They specify, so to speak, a general schedule of social coordination. This schedule of activities is related to the orientational system of the role. The symbolic stabilization of this orientation is further anchored in relating it to a cultural context relevant to the role activities. This is especially obvious in the case of the professional roles. The implication is that the role provides role typical perspectives, which consist of culturally available epistemologies, preference systems, theories and methodologies.

Roles as Orientation Systems

Roles must be thought of as providing the central *social* arrangement of reality constructs and their structure must, thus, be related to the structure of the frames of reference and theories held by the role occupants. Roles may, indeed, be viewed as frames of reference and theories in terms of which the role occupants deal with the situations which come their way. It may be an unconventional way of phrasing the matter, but it is, nevertheless, quite evident: social roles in their orientational function provide epistemologies, basic categorical schemes, preference systems, and methodologies through which the role occupant organizes the encountered experiences and provides explanations for them. A mode of analysis usually reserved by the intellectual historian to the social role of the highly accomplished man of knowledge, such as philosophers or scientists, must by extension be applied to the roles enacted by the "common folk." The guard in a zoo, the administrator in a complex organization, the plumber, all possess more or less specialized frames of reference and explanatory theories which presumably equip them to do their jobs.

Each design for a work performance, such as the organizational blueprints decided upon by the administrator, or the plumber's plan for repairing a fixture, and the like, constitute the application of theories not only in the explanatory, but even in the predictive sense. The users commit themselves heavily to the actual attainment of the desired outcome which the theory implicitly or explicitly predicts.

Role-specific frames of reference must be anchored in the legitimation of the social role itself, but they also must permit the construction and application of workable theories. The theories built into social roles thus are influenced by two sets of constraints: role-specific frames of reference are limited by the legitimation of the social role itself, but also by the actually encountered situations. The frame of reference of a role reflects the social location of the role in both the orientational and situational sense.

The social location of the role is fixed with reference to institutional spheres and loyalty structures of a society. "Institutional spheres" are sets of interrelated values and corresponding social activities which cluster around socially recognized tasks. Institutional spheres often are more or less formally organized; this is particularly true in the "public domain." The extent of formal organization, however, is a matter of wide variation. Examples of institutional spheres include the business sphere, the political-administrative sphere, the religious sphere, the military sphere, the educational sphere, and other domains. The organization of an institutional sphere can be characterized in terms of its specific value system which provides the most general rationale for action within it. It further involves the actually operative social relationships which, together with the values institutionalized within the sphere, determine its dynamics. The concept "institutional dynamics" may be a useful term to refer to the social changes which result from the specialization and clarification of the value purposes of an institutional sphere.

Within institutional spheres, social action is guided by the frames of reference and epistemologies which are broadly set by the values and by the more or less specific theories which deal with the "demands" of situational tasks. Each institutional sphere, then, can be treated as a subsystem of society, providing its own impetus for change or stability, the direction of which may be in conflict with the impetus for change resulting from other spheres within the same society. The specific social location of a role within an institutional sphere can be plotted on something like a "map" of the differentiation within and among institutional spheres generally. In order to understand the location of a role, the interrelation among institutional domains must be clarified, especially with regard to the strategic positions which may give one or more domains dominance over others. In their internal structure, the specific relationship among the roles within the sphere is also significant. It is particularly necessary to understand the special value systems underlying the institutional sphere, and their relation to the values of other domains. The special value system within a sphere describes in a most general sense the system of action orientations found in this domain of society. More specifically, it also determines a legitimate way of evaluating positions, their rank and their differential authority. Each institutional sphere, then, has to some extent its own legitimate distribution of authority and rank which provides one structure for the "stratification" of roles.

A given role-specific frame of reference usually will also relate to the groupings into which the role occupant is generally integrated. Here the concern is with a person's loyalties and memberships. "Loyalty" is simply the socially positive side of personal identity, and group loyalties provide the structured distribution and the organization of such social identities. Institutional spheres, naturally, may give rise to certain role identifications and loyalties but rarely do they become the central focus of felt and expressed loyalty. There are groupings which often cut across different institutional spheres, providing one form of integration of the society. The action orientation constitutive of loyalties to groups is composed of personal commitments and emotional identifications; it is not, as in the institutional spheres, primarily focused on the exigencies of dealing with cultural objects and work situations. A given social role, however, will tend to be defined in terms of both institutional and loyalty commitments. One must attempt to find the roots of its specific frame of reference in both aspects of social relations.

The discussion has shown that there is a strong relationship between the frame of reference of a social role, and the values of institutional spheres and social groupings into which it is placed. The tendency of these structural units of a society to drift into the direction of comprehensive and isolative values respectively is strong. The demands of solving socially recognized tasks in the institutional spheres make for an emphasis on comprehensive values, which is quite different from the drift toward isolative values in bounded groups, which results from the experience of social boundaries on one side, and of belonging on the other. These tendencies provide strong determinants of the variation in the role specific frames of reference and in the substantive theories which are acceptable. They also make for affinities among social roles.

The activities and the orientations of role occupants must relate to those of others; there is an interplay between roles as orientation systems and roles as social objects. In this interplay actual transactions are accomplished, even where the relationship between the orientation of one role occupant and that of another is one of disparity. It is true, there must be a shared base of understanding the situation for the interaction to proceed at all. But the actual degree of similarity in the frames of reference with which role occupants approach the situation is a matter of wide variation. There are several possibilities here: the first one is the complete identity, or a high degree of similarity of the orientation systems. Fellow believers in a common faith, persons with the same occupation and training may be illustrations of this category. Most actual transactions in society invoke some dissimilarities of orientation; but the cases of identity of orientation systems are especially interesting, from the point of view of the social distribution of reality constructs. Where we find such similarity of frames of reference, of epistemologies, we find naturally also agreement on the application of similar reality tests. In the case of organized social arrangements which maintain such similar epistemologies we may speak of "epistemic communities," such as that of science, of an organized religion, an ideological following and the like.

A second possibility in the relations of orientation systems is that of a very high degree of dissimilarity, ranging from the case of total and systematic misunderstanding to the case of highly segmental, and regularized relations. Total misunderstanding, the systematic misreading of the other's view of the situation, is probably more frequent in social life than is generally assumed. Political life offers many illustrations of the phenomenon; but we find it in other domains, too. The difficulties which many psychiatrists appear to encounter in the psychotherapeutic treatment of lower class persons may be used as another example. Where frames of reference are disparate, but transactions are of necessity frequent, as in the case of many laymen's relations to some expert, a supporting framework of social arrangements tends to arise which limits and structures the interaction context. Misunderstandings continue to occur, but the limitations in the scope of interaction, and the distribution of power within it channel them so that their consequences remain socially acceptable.

A third possibility is that of the case in which one of the interaction partners "understands" the other, without the reverse being true. The orientation system of the first agent can be said to encompass that of the other, whereas the other misconstrues the orientation system of the first agent. In these cases great manipulative power falls into the hands of the knowledgeable person.

The Establishment of Epistemic Communities

The meshing of highly similar role orientations is essential for the establishment of epistemic communities. We are dealing here with those at least partially interlinked roles which are unified by a common epistemology and frame of reference, such as the scientific community, religious communities, work communities, some ideological movements and the like. All members of such a community, in their capacity as members agree on "the" proper perspective for the construction of reality. In these communities the conditions of reliability and validity of reality constructs are known and the applicable standards are shared. Within such epistemic communities we may thus speak of truly shared modes of the construction of reality; rarely is such sharing established on a society-wide basis. In fact, in the differentiated society of the industrial age it is especially obvious that any individual is likely to participate in various ways in different epistemic communities to which he is linked by his roles and through channels of communication. The diversity in his own modes of reality construction is, then, directly linked to the scope of diversity of epistemic communities.

The establishment of the shared frames of reference characteristic of epistemic communities is a delicate process. There is not only the requirement of value congruency among the participants, but moreover the need for power arrangements in the exchanges of the interaction processes which sustain the shared perspective once it is established, or influence its acceptance in the first place. We did see that power is an integral aspect of all interaction; the significance of power relationships in the growth and maintenance of epistemic communities is illustrated by the high level of power consciousness which can be observed (even though it is sometimes disguised) in nearly all professional groups, and certainly in most ideological movements. The sociology of epistemic communities must in large measure be concerned with the frames of reference and epistemologies themselves, but it must relate such facts immediately to the realities of interaction patterns, including the power structures sustaining them.

Epistemic communities, once established as power structures, tend to regulate not only the frames of reference or orientations of their members, but they also concern themselves with the regulation of the allocation of situations to the members. The assignment of tasks on the basis of certified expertise is merely the most clear-cut example. The relationships with the surrounding society are a matter of grave importance to such communities; the careful management of information flow out of the epistemic community can often be understood in the context of power structures and attempts at controlling the situations which members must face. One aid in the process is the tendency to standardize the symbolic system used within the community in such a way that it becomes separate and distinct. In many instances the barriers which flow naturally from such separateness are reinforced by conscious attempts to keep certain knowledge secret, hidden from the view of the ordinary man. Whatever the specific constellation of these factors may be which we might find in a particular epistemic community, there are certain quite general principles which hold true across the great diversity of epistemic communities; the importance of the interplay among the structure of the frame of reference, the symbolic system used within, and the power arrangements of the epistemic community are among them. The consequences of differentiation in socially organized modes of reality construction for the role of "common man" are another general feature: there are relatively few different ways in which the common man can be linked to the variety of epistemic communities in his society.

From the epistemological point of view the critical difference among epistemic communities lies in the nature of the experiential base on which their reality constructs rest, and in the principles of equivalence or nonequivalence of observers within the relevant domain. The experiential base of the reality construct was described in the previous chapter in a typology: the pragmatic tests of experienced workability, the logical test of deductive establishment of "truth," the mystical test of personal insight, and the test by authority, or alienation. It is evident that in the case of the first two types of reality test observers are, in principle, interchangeable. In the case of the latter two instances this interchangeability usually does not exist.

Observer equivalence is, of course, the prevailing principle in science and the science related work communities. It is qualified, to be sure, in that the observer must establish his proper credentials as a person holding the required frame of reference and using the prescribed symbolic system. But in principle these and other prerequisites are believed to be learnable so that all men, given proper preparation, are seen as qualified. One competent observer is as good, in principle, as another observer. In fact, the scientific enterprise is built on the requirement of intersubjective verification of observations; experiences which are *in principle* only accessible to one person are outside the proper domain of science. This does not negate the fact that one man, who happens to observe a natural phenomenon which no other before him saw, may be a qualified observer and his observation may be properly within the domain of science: if it is not *in principle* private.

It is clear that the internal structure of epistemic communities which are built upon the principle of observer equivalence must necessarily be different from the internal structure of those epistemic communities which are built upon the principle of non-equivalence, or the belief in some especially privileged observers. The religious prophet, or the inspired charismatic leader of an ideological movement are believed to have superior powers of insight; they may be viewed as having access to sources of knowledge inaccessible to others. The superior power of vision in the man of "higher qualities" is widely believed in certain types of epistemic communities, and it becomes itself an aspect of their mode of reality construction.

Broadly, the principles of observer equivalence or non-equivalence relate to the work and logic based reality tests on one side, and the identity and authority based reality tests on the other. We found the social organization of work and of authority to be the matter of the greatest importance for the understanding of reality constructs. It is clear that working communities will tend toward the application of work related reality tests in the context of observer equivalence, whereas ideological communities will tend in the opposite direction. These are issues which we will explore in detail in the last part of this book.

Chapter V

The Construction of Social Structure

Two Aspects of Social Structure

Social structure, the relatively stable patterns of relationships, of roles, groups, institutions in society, must be understood as an achievement resulting from the process of constructive stabilization of the fluent interactive process. We have emphasized the importance of symbolic representation for this "construction of social structure," which provides some firm anchorage points for the orientation of an individual to his social environment. The process includes more than the orderliness made possible by symbolic orientation; it involves further the coordination of overt action, and the regulation of situations in which the action takes place.

We may distinguish two aspects of social structure in this regard. One of these arises when society is viewed from the perspective of the conscious, participating observer. Putting it simply, we can say that from this point of view society is seen as a vast network of interconnected subjects. However, from the point of view of the detached viewer, it may appear as a large number of interdependent objects in motion. In the first view, society consists of the images which its members have of it, their beliefs about social reality, their views of each other, of their roles, of the roles of their partners, their knowledge of groups, organizations, and of institutions that have some importance for them. The subject-agents who make up society in this view know norms, such as laws, customs, and the like, which regulate their behavior. They legitimize their actions in terms of values, such as the value of freedom, of equality, of saintliness, of honour, or whatever else it may be. All of these images of social life, known norms, and legitimizing values, relate to the orientations of people who observe social life in the context in which they themselves act. We thus will call this first aspect of society the orientational one. The structure of society which emerges if one traces the interlocking perspectives or orientations of its members, we will call the "orientational structure."

The other point of view yields a different picture in that a detached observer who by choice ignores the individual orientations of those he observes obtains a view of society as a distribution of persons, activities, and environments or settings. It involves transactions in the course of which objects move from one agent to another, and distances are overcome. Objects, be they facilities, or rewards, or information, or persons, move through the territory in which a society exists. We see that actions must be performed by certain people at specific times and at specific places because they are linked with the activities of others at other times and in other places. In other words, from this perspective there emerges a picture of the manifold situations which confront conscious agents and their distribution in time and space. It is rather similar to the picture which the student of any organismic environment obtains.

We thus call this second aspect of society the "situational" one, describing the characteristics and interconnections among the environments faced by different people. The term "environment" in this context, however, must not be taken in its simple, physicalistic sense. Objects that are of significance in social environments are often cultural objects, and always culturally defined ones; our interest thus concerns the distribution of culturally more or less standardized situations, and their allocation to people.

The characteristics of these two aspects require further study. We begin with the orientational aspects. Let us focus on the example of an interpersonal encounter. One may think, for example, of conversations, of the making of acquaintances and other everyday situations like them. In all such situations, be they simple or complex, we can easily see that the understandings which the participants form of each other, of themselves, and of the enveloping social arrangements, are essential for the course of the social encounter itself. In fact, it is quite justified to say that such understandings or misunderstandings, as the case may be, are constitutive of the social encounter at least in part.

There appears to emerge an apparent paradox out of these considerations: The social reality of interactions is, at least in part, constituted by the participants' views of it. George Simmel found a most incisive formulation of this matter in his essay "How is Society Possible?" With the assertion that cognitive "syntheses" are the basis of the social process, he expressed the very theme which we try to capture with the concept of the "orientational structure" of society. It is worth our while to digress a little to follow Simmel's thoughts.

He reminds us that Kant raised the question of how the conception and understanding of nature become possible. It was Kant's great insight to discover that nature is nothing but the "representation of nature." This must be understood not only in the sense that nature, as we know it, is always a content of our consciousness so that one could say, generally, that "the world is my representation." But for Kant it was even more important to see that our understanding of nature arises in the special way in which the human mind assembles, orders, and shapes our sense perceptions.

The perceptions themselves arise and pass through our consciousness in the accidental sequence of our own subjective experience. In themselves the perceptions would be confused, and certainly are not yet what we mean by "nature." "They rather become nature, and they do so through the activity of the mind which combines them into objects and series of objects, into substances and attributes, and into causal connections. In their immediate givenness, Kant held, the elements of the world do not have the interdependence which alone makes them intelligible as the unity of nature's laws. It is this interdependence which transforms the world fragments — in themselves incoherent and unstructured — into nature."

Simmel continues: " . . . it is very suggestive to treat as an analogous matter the question of the aprioristic conditions under which society is possible. Here, also, we find individual elements. In a certain sense, they too, like sense perceptions, stay forever isolated from one another. They likewise, are synthesized into the unity of society only by means of a conscious process which correlates the individual existence of the single element with that of the other, and does so in certain forms and according to certain rules. However, there is a decisive difference between the unity of society and the unity of nature. It is this: in the Kantian view (which we follow here), the unity of nature emerges in the observing subject exclusively; it is produced exclusively by him in the sense materials and on the basis of the sense materials, which are in themselves heterogeneous. By contrast, the unity of society needs no observer. It is directly realized by its own elements because these elements are themselves conscious and synthesizing units. Kant's axiom that connection, since it is the exclusive product of the subject, cannot inhere in things themselves, does not apply here. For societal connection immediately occurs in the "things," that is the individuals."*

Society, for Simmel, exists in the relations of conscious individuals, in the reciprocal but usually asymmetrical cognitions and in the resulting interactions among such conscious agents. It exists, in other words, in the interplay of cognitive perspectives as well as in the concrete actions which the members of society perform. Thus society is, in Simmel's view, fundamentally cognitive in nature. He gives what we call the orientational aspect of society distinctive priority over the situational aspect, even though certain situational, especially numerically distributive facts fascinate him. In applying the Kantian method to the study of society, Simmel discovers the fact that every member of society creates, in a way, one aspect of the unity of his society as a whole through his understanding of the social relationships in which he is involved, and through his conception of the social structure into which he is placed. Simmel's society includes a variety of cognitive perspectives, those of "actors" and "objects," and "I" and "You," of "self" and "other," of "We" and "They." In this sense, then, social knowledge, knowledge of self, of others, of groups, of institutions, of norms, is constitutive of society itself. Social cohesion is fundamentally constituted by the sharedness of social meanings, or, we could say, society consists of "agent-observers:" persons who act and observe, and observe and act. Modifying Simmel: one level of the unity of society can be observed in its members' cognitions of it.

Simmel, then, argues that Kant showed nature, or the laws of nature to be "synthesized" or created by the human observer. It is the observer who creates through categories and explanatory systems organized unity of the manifold of inherently unorganized sense perceptions. In society, however, every member, being an observer himself, performs this synthesis. For Kant, nature has to be "synthesized" within the frame of

*George Simmel, "How is Society Possible?" in *George Simmel 1858-1918*, Kurt Wolff, editor, Columbus, Ohio, The Ohio State University Press, 1959, p. 337.

reference of the necessary forms of intuition, time and space, and in terms of the categories, which he derived from the structure of the different types of propositions known to logic.

Simmel, by analogy, seeks to find "sociological aprioris." These would be the necessary forms of the social "synthesis." Today, we must admit, this method no longer sounds promising to social scientists. We know too well that the cognitive perspectives in the context of which persons develop, elaborate, and express their views of social realities, vary widely and cannot be reduced to a simple, neat, symmetrical table of categories in the Kantian fashion.

It is at this point that we must recognize an encompassing relationship between fundamental properties of cognitive processes and the structuring of social systems. Culturally crystallized frames of reference shape the type constructs of social roles, of relationships, groups, and societies. They give rise to general tendencies in the forming of images of society, which in turn become guidelines of social action. A society, possessing a common culture and language, thus is likely to develop a pervasive cognitive style which enters into the myriad implicit and explicit decisions and actions which structure the ongoing processes of the social system. These fundamental relationships are not well understood, but we must be aware of them; they are epitomized by the notion that "values," which always have a cognitive component, are the supreme structuring principles in the social process.

There is, then, a pervasive context within which the specific structuring of society into role types takes place. We however, must concern ourselves later in this book in greater detail with the specific differentiation of the orientational structure of society, leaving the encompassing issues of the function of values and their concomitant cognitive styles in the background.

Orientations function in the context of situations. While Kant assumed that the sequence and structure of "sensations" and "perceptions" might well be random in itself, we know that in the context of social life experiences are not randomly encountered by people. Independently of the organizing power of the orientations with which persons approach and interpret their experience, society regulates and limits their exposure to potential experience itself. This consideration turns our attention to the "situational structure" of the social system.

Emile Durkheim in his book, *The Division of Labor in Society,** grapples with the issue of how basically different patterns of social differentiation and integration relate to the normative structure of society and the well-being of the social organism and its members. In this enterprise he develops an image of society which closely approximates what we have in mind when we speak of society's situational aspect. His society produces through the operation of its many and variously interdependent "organs" sets of constraints which are external to its members and compel their behavior.

The concrete constraints facing different individuals are distributed in the whole system of the society by means of a complex and delicately regulated machinery which in certain cases can be shown to have broken down. It then produces an "anomic" state, originally understood by Durkheim as a state of social life in which these regulations external to the individual collapse. The basic image of society is well illustrated by Durkheim's analysis of the limitations of the regulative role of government in relation to the multiple interdependencies of the division of labor.

He discusses the regulative role of government which seems to him merely a small, visible aspect of societal regulation in general. ". . .beneath this general, superficial life, there is an intestine, a world of organs, which, without being completely independent of the first, nevertheless functions without its intervention, without its even being conscious of them, at least normally.** It's simply not possible for government to intervene in all the myriad interconnections and conditions of society. It cannot regulate all the conditions pertinent to the economic markets, matching consumption and production, and fixing all prices. This is, in the last analysis, impossible even if it is attempted because of the remoteness of the intentional regulative agencies. "All these practical problems arise from a multitude of detail, coming from thousands of particular circumstances which only those very close to the problem know of."*** If

*Emile Durkheim, *The Division of Labor in Society*, translated by George Simpson, The Free Press of Glencoe, Illinois, copyright 1933 by MacMillan Company, 4th printing, 1960.
**op. cit. p. 360
***ibid.

these many, detail functions do not mesh harmoniously by themselves, they cannot easily be adjusted to each other. "If then, the
division of labor has the dispersive effects that are attributed
to it, they ought to develop without resistance in this region of
society, since there is nothing to hold them together. What
gives unity to organized societies, however, as to all organisms,
is the spontaneous consensus of parts. Such is the internal solidarity which not only is as indispensable as the regulative action
of higher centers, but which also is their necessary condition, for
they do no more than translate it into another language and, so
to speak, consecrate it."*

Durkheim projects here, in the explicit language of the organismic analogy, an image of society as a vast and complex
mechanism that regulates and distributes the flow of goods, of
information, of persons, quite independently of almost any conscious plans or interference. Governmental planning may be a
small aspect of this process. He sees society, we could say, almost as a vast mechanism that provides the "objective"settings in which any given individual must necessarily operate.
The difference from Simmel's view is large and obvious; but,
yet, the two complement each other. Durkheim is at this stage
of his sociological thinking concerned with the external events
which the Simmelian approach must take as the basic "manifold
of experience" which is transformed into a meaningful order
through "synthesis." Durkheim emphasized the "situational" aspect of social structure more than the "orientational" one (at
the stage of the "Division of Labor" book).

We must recognize that human habitats or situations are not
describable in purely physical and biological terms. They are
assigned standard cultural meanings; they confront their inhab-
itants with situations that demand something of them, such as
"housekeeping situations," or "shopping situations," or "working
situations," and the like. Such situations are socially and culturally defined, but since their meanings are socially standardized,
they are largely independent of the particular individual confronting them.

Another illustration of a sociologist describing the situational
aspect of society can be found in a paper by Talcott Parsons. As
is well known, the bulk of his work tends to emphasize the
orientational aspect of social life, but, in this paper Parsons at-

**op. cit., p. 360

tempts to deal with the concept "community" as an analytical category.* He sees this concept as referring to "that aspect of the structure of social systems which is referrable to the territorial location of persons (i.e., human individuals as organisms) and their activities. When I say "referrable to," I do not mean determined exclusively or predominantly by, but rather observable and analyzable with reference to location as a focus of attention (and, of course, a partial determinant). In this respect the study of community structures comes close to what an important group of sociologists (centering in the University of Chicago and later of Michigan) have called the "ecological approach" to the study of social phenomena. Though the territorial reference is central, it should also be pointed out that there is another term to the relation. The full formula then comprises persons acting in territorial locations, and since the reference is to social relations, persons acting in relation to other persons in respect to the territorial location of both parties. The population, then, is just as much a focus of the study of community, as is the territorial location."**

Parsons' emphasis on the social action nature of "ecological" relations makes his view of the matter come closest to ours. As the rest of his paper makes clear, he is indeed studying the occurrence of activities, the flow of information, goods and people, as they relate to and distribute over space and time.

The foregoing quotes make clear, I think, that the situational aspect of society comes into view if the observer looks upon social activity as constrained by and producing things which are distributed in space and time. It becomes obvious that the environments which are significant to and constraining upon different individuals are differentially distributed. If we take the population as our referent, we may say that such environments are differentially allocated to the individuals by the situational structure of the society. Such, for example, is the meaning of sociological talk about the "life chances" which an individual may or may not enjoy due to his position in the stratified order. A lower class person finds himself in a different habitat from an upper class person, and as a consequence, events, situations

*Chapter 8, The Principal Structures of Community, pp. 250-279 in Talcott Parsons, *Structure and Process in Modern Societies,* The Free Press of Glencoe, Illinois, 1960.
**op. cit. pp. 250-251.

which he is likely to face, are different from those faced by the upper class person. More specifically, even, the fully trained and positioned medical professional will find himself in a habitat confronting situations, which the situational structure of society channels his way, which differ drastically from the situations encountered by a steel worker. The complex machinery that regulates the flow of such situations is the machinery that Durkheim alluded to in our quotation.

To sum it up: society appears as a multitude of timed and spaced situations which define the living environments of individuals who are, also, distributed in space and time.

The fact that the orientational and situational aspects of society are merely two different sides of the same object, appearing to the observer from different perspectives, immediately forces us to recognize the serious problem of their interdependencies. Orientations and the distribution of situations must mesh, not only for the sake of the individual agent, but even more so for the viability of the system as a whole, so that it may operate effectively. We now turn to the issue of coordination implied in this fact.

The Coordination of Orientational and Situational Structure

The basic coordination between the orientational and situational structures of a society occurs in the shared framework of space and time which the society establishes for its collective life. In the previous discussion we pointed to the fact that experienced space is structured through outstanding landmarks and the distances between them that must be overcome in the context of some activity. Experiential space thus relates to the physical signs that are of significance in the context of an orientational structure. It is necessarily "distorted" when compared to the distribution of physical objects which might be mapped by the detached observer in terms of the coordinates of longitude and latitude.

Experiential spaces are thus as diverse as the many individuals composing a population. They necessarily must be coordinated. It cannot be simply a matter of the idiosyncratic experiential world of this or that person: communities, societies must necessarily arrange their activities over a given territory and must coordinate their interrelations on this base. There are, therefore, shared "maps" of the encompassing community that articulate with the experiential spaces of all subgroups and the individual members. Such shared "maps" require, in the most simple case, highly visible landmarks that enter into all experiential spaces contained within the community. In the case of large territories and differentiated societies, the specialized management of space and orientation in space become an important activity, for instance, in technology. The specialized spatial framework of natural science is, of course, the result of experience in the same way. It is, however, a carefully standardized experience, that imposes on all observers the same perspective and the same language and thus makes the construction of a uniform space conception possible.

Similarly, we discussed, before, the requirement for the synchronization and coordination of experiential time. Time is experienced as a duration between significant events, some of which recur so that they act as landmarks in the structuring of recurring time. One observes this process most clearly in traditional societies in which the flow of time is not measured by physical devices. Here the sequence of the seasons and the regular activities which correspond to the seasons (e.g., the festivals that mark the calendar and define it, or the sequence of socially shared activities throughout the day) set the major landmarks for the orientation in recurring time, just as birth, death, and the sequence of generations set the landmarks in non-recurring time.

Experiential time again can be shown to be distorted over physically measured time. Everybody knows from his own experience that activity-filled periods appear of short duration and that physically shorter time periods spent in waiting for a significant event may appear much longer. Temporal landmarks thus come to be of special significance; they, too, must fill the requirement of being widely visible and entering into the experiential times of all relevant persons. To some extent this is facilitated by the natural synchronization of similar life functions and activities. More significant, however, is the fact that social groups, in "managing" the activities of their members, manage the frameworks of perceived time for them as well. It is a common observation that separated institutions or organizations, such as jails or isolated schools, define for their inmates or members temporal landmarks which differ from the temporal landmarks used in the surrounding communities. The management of experiential time thus can be an instrument of social coordination to the extent of helping to sustain group boundaries.

Within these landmark studded extensions of social space and social time, societies construct the shared picture of the world and individuals define their experiential worlds. It is within these shared contexts that social situations are defined. The conception of space and time thus forms the basis for the coordination of the physical flow of persons, information, and material through the social structure, as well as for the elaboration of the orientational structure that the society develops. The final stage of abstract space, of time as measured by the clock or in the physical experiment, can be experientially sustained only over short periods by the concrete, living individual. It essentially runs "alongside" experiential time and space, only connected to it at some points. It becomes clear that the maintenance of the elaborate spatial-temporal organization upon which the complex society with its intricate requirements for social coordination is based, needs the careful institutionalization of specific orientations toward space and time.

In the context of this time-space framework social differentiation takes place by elaborating both appropriate role orientations and roles as schedules for timed and spaced activities. In a sense these schedules of activities which fit into the actually arising situations, provide a most significant, albeit general "test" for the relevant orientational structures and beliefs. Symbolic conceptions of relationships, of communication channels, of transaction processes are elaborated and relate the differentiated regions of the social structure to each other. These conceptions of relationships must mesh with the actual occurrence of timed and spaced interconnections, at least to the extent of compatibility with the actual "scheduling" of events.

The orientational structure of society and the actual allocation of situations must, then, be coordinated in the sense that the time-space orientations of people must mesh, at least at critical points, with the actual distribution of events and activities, and in the sense that conceptions of relationships, of communication channels, of transactions must correspond at least roughly with the processes they represent. We find far-reaching parallels in the analysis of coordination and the structuring of orientation systems themselves.

Yet, the requirement of coordination only touches upon the

most obvious and basic issues. It is necessary to realize that beyond this basic level the orientational framework of any role must mesh with the situations to be dealt with by the role occupant not merely in the sense that he can "place" himself in space and time and can successfully apply the "reality tests" (which we discussed above) to the phenomena he experiences. He must achieve a level of mastery over the situations he deals with which permits not only his perceptions of reality in "correct" ways, but also leads him to perform adequately. In fact, we may have to recognize that the shaping of reality tests, and the social definition of their appropriateness, depends on this encompassing criterion: do they lead to or are they at least compatible with socially workable solutions to the situational problems? Mystical, or authoritative tests which violate the rules of empirical evidence find their ultimate support in the interdependencies of the ongoing social system; in a different way the permissibility of empirical tests, where it occurs, is supported by these contexts.

A problem of coordination of particular interest to us, even though it is an issue of limited scope, is the coordination of different modes of reality construction relative to one situation which demands a binding decision. Examples abound for these processes in differentiated societies: a court of law is charged with the responsibility to determine "the facts" in a case, and to arrive at a definitive judgment in accord with the law. The court may hear many witnesses, including experts of widely varying kinds. It is interesting to note that the frames of reference, the methodologies, the theories, even the reality tests of the experts from medicine, psychiatry, psychology, social work, and possibly from one of the specialties of natural science and so on, differ in many fundamental respects. The court must assign to them their specific tasks, and their relative weight. The intricate system of social organization which coordinates different frames of reference, different epistemic communities, at the point of action in the concrete situation, is epitomized by this example. Any other example of "consultation" would serve as well: the sociological problem of coordinating different epistemic communities in the situational context is a general one.

The encompassing power structures of a society, and the scope of regulated authority play a central role in the processes of coordinating epistemic communities with relation to specific situational problems. In fact, "power" as the ability to control the activities of others and to influence the distribution of situations is the strategic aspect of the coordination process which must be analyzed for an understanding of how the allocation of situations and orientations mesh. The term "power" is used by us quite as broadly as we defined it; it may take a number of different forms, of which direct, coercive power is only one. We will remain sensitive to the significance of power in relation to modes of reality construction throughout our discussion. Here the interdependence between social structure and reality construction comes particularly close to the surface. Where power is consciously exercised, it rests on the development of effective social strategies for manipulation and the attainment of goals. These strategies themselves reflect modes of reality construction, and may, in fact, rest on a "monopoly of knowledge" which gives its holder a great advantage over others.

This brings us to the conclusion of the first part of our discussion in which we dealt with the "processes of reality construction" and their general relations to the experience of the individual on one side and to social structure on the other. We have addressed ourselves to the first two, broad problem areas of the sociology of knowledge: the socio-cultural shaping of reality construction, and the relations of modes of reality construction to social structuring in general. The next part of this essay will deal, albeit briefly, with three pervasive aspects of the distribution and control of reality constructs and modes of reality construction in social systems.

Part II

THREE ASPECTS OF REALITY CONSTRUCTION IN SOCIAL SYSTEMS: ORIENTATIONS, SITUATIONS, AND COMMUNICATIONS

Chapter VI

The Social Distribution and Control of Orientations

The basic fact of the differentiated distribution of orientations has been discussed in previous chapters. It underlies the conception of the orientational structure of a society; its significance has been abundantly documented both with regard to the minute differentiation of specific roles and the gross distribution of values, points of view, ideologies, political "cleavages" and other social phenomena. The structured distribution of orientations is so basic and fundamental a social phenomenon that its influence has been demonstrated in many respects far less obvious than those just listed, such as in the distribution and epidemiology of mental illness, the differential utilization of medical services by persons in different social locations and in a multitude of other aspects of social life. It must even be said, as the discussions of the previous chapters showed, that the orientations of persons are constitutive of society; their relations to the situational structure is one of our major problems.

A full discussion of a society's orientational structure thus would require the detailed analysis of virtually every facet of social life; such a task is beyond us. It is fruitful, however, to highlight a selected number of especially important aspects in the distribution and control of orientations.

Social and Cultural Horizons

One of the most basic facts which strikes the observer of any society is the limitation of cultural and social horizons of its people. One may differentiate between these closely related concepts: (1) the cultural horizon limits the range of cultural meanings, (for example, values, frames of reference, explanatory theories or specific items of information) which are accessible to the occupant of a given position; (2) the social horizon bounds the range of knowledge about the society and its structure which is accessible to the occupant of a given position.

There is a temporal aspect to both "horizons" which is expressed in the often vaguely used notion of "Zeitgeist." Due to the state of culture in a particular period, often influenced by the authoritative word of the "experts," any period is characterized by a typical limitation of basic orientations and specific theories available in the culture as a whole. The determinants of this phenomenon are various and complex; some of them are discussed in later chapters—especially when the analysis focuses on the problem of the authoritative "freezing" of working theories into normatively sanctioned positions.

One may think, for example, of the vogue of biologistic theories of human behavior in the late nineteenth and early twentieth centuries, as against the dominance of environmentalist theories in the Western cultures of the present. The current state of scientific, philosophical, religious knowledge, the preferences in literature and the arts are major influences on the cultural horizons of any historical period. In fact the very prominence and salience of certain points of view may be linked with highly visible personalities or groups who tend to limit the range of alternatives available. Similar phenomena occur in the social horizons; there are always limited alternatives among the models of society in terms of which a person may arrange what he knows or thinks he knows about his groups. Such images of society may be highly elaborate, as they were, for example, in the major ideologies of the nineteenth century, or they may be extremely simplistic. In their orientational function they do, in any case, restrict the scope of information about society taken into account and thus they influence the social horizon itself.

The temporal aspect of social and cultural horizons reflects directly the dynamics of socio-cultural change. But within any time period further differentiations of "horizons" can be found which link them to the nature of social positions. Every student of social stratification has remarked upon the fact that members of different social strata have a sometimes drastically different range of culture and of social information within their reach. In fact, one may in this connection speak of subcultures and subsocieties which crystallize around the differentiation of a society into status groups, castes, or classes. The social horizons of the very lowest classes tend to be so limited that the image they hold of the highest ones becomes blurred and fused. The reverse frequently holds as well because higher strata may be entirely ignorant of the conditions prevailing among the lower social layers. They may, indeed, be ignorant of some of the most basic facts of social differentiation. There is little doubt that on the whole the social and cultural horizons of the upper strata are broader in scope, include a wider range of information than those of lower strata. There are, however, knowledges and beliefs peculiar to lower strata which may give their subculture a richness and differentiation which the uninformed observer may even fail to suspect.

To describe the differentiation of a society merely in terms of social stratification is really a limited and indeed a very crude approach; it has its obvious uses, but a closer look is indicated. There are institutional spheres and loyalty structures which may differentiate social positions within as well as among strata. Peculiar subcultures develop within the major institutional spheres. One may think, for example, of the subculture of business in the United States, or of the social and cultural horizons open to those whose roles involve them in the educational institutions. Occupational roles are today especially important determinants of access to social knowledge and cultural goods. The country parson in a small Mid-western town may not know very much about nuclear physics or about the sociology of knowledge, but he will have a more detailed picture of his particular community and of his church than the great physicist could possibly possess.

All of these facts are fairly obvious once they are mentioned. And yet, social scientists have often enough neglected them, even to the point of underestimating the potent differentiation of social-cultural horizons by one's relations to loyalty structures. Nationality and ethnicity, religious affiliation and many other group memberships tend to provide foci of commitments around which the known world is organized and information availability is restricted. They tend to focus collective interests for knowledge on group relevant areas. In short the differentiation of both social and cultural horizons reflects the very differentiation of society itself; it is related to the communication network and the situational structure.

At the same time, "horizons" cannot be treated as *mere* attributes of social positions which are set by the social structure. Any person's cultural horizon depends, to be sure, on what aspects of the collective culture he is almost automatically and necessarily exposed to. But it also depends on the scope and nature of his personal interests. There is, thus, an active as well as passive aspect to these "horizons." They are interdependent with the nature of a person's experiences in the course of his socialization and personality development, with his education and with the requirements of his role. In fact the arousal of expanded interests in social facts during a collective crisis may well expand the social horizon to encompass aspects of the society previously neglected by a person, or the immediate and personal crisis may contract it.

The differentiation of social and cultural horizons, then, would be determined most directly by the particular structuring of a society into institutional spheres and loyalty structures, especially as they channel the flow of communication. But there are also indirect effects through the variation of socialization patterns in different areas of the social structure. Further, we must single out the nature and the scope of the authority system which will tend to connect some members of the group to the centrally operative structures, while possibly excluding others. It may also give rise to the deliberate strategic manipulation of cultural horizons through censorship and repression, maybe even through conscious lies—as the prominent enlightenment theory suggested which alleged deliberate fraud on the part of the priests to mislead the masses. There are, thus, links which connect the phenomenon of differentiated "horizons" and their characteristic ties to social positions, to the other problems of the distribution of situations and the channeling of communications. It is this linkage which makes the relation of "horizons" to the social stratification system so obvious.

In any case, the limiting of cultural alternatives and social knowledge through the restricted scope of cultural and social horizons in itself is a most powerful instrument in the control of orientations. This is one reason why simple culture contact has so often been mentioned as an important source of social change: it expands the cultural horizons and opens up alternatives of thought and action undreamed of before.

Socialization and Education

The second general and basic fact making for a differential distribution of orientations throughout a society lies in the pattern of socialization. The social and cultural horizons, as well as the specific institutional structure of families that share social locations, tend to standardize socialization patterns at the same time that they differentiate them from those prevalent in other areas of the social structure. There is a most direct and straightforward connection between the images of society and the development of persons, in that these persons must find their roles somewhere located in the society as they understand it. The limitation of "horizons" thus limits the range of social goals, sometimes leading to the systematic indoctrination of children to strive for realistically unattainable goals. Similarly straightforward may be the transmission of beliefs and values prevalent in the subculture. But there are important indirect results of socialization. The very landmark structure of the cognitive world which a person develops in the socialization process possibly implies major discrepancies between persons coming from different social locations, leading to unanticipated gaps and links between different social personality types.

The outcomes of the interactions between the socialization situation and the general dynamics of the growing personality are a further basis for significant differentiation in orientations. Some attempts have been made to account for myths and beliefs entirely on the basis of their functional value to relieve stresses and strains in the emotional structure of the personalities which are being variously pressed and pushed to fit a social mold.

In complex societies the shaping of orientations and the transmission of knowledge and skills are the most explicit concerns of educational institutions and organizations. The separation of educational tasks to constitute the focus of a distinct institutional sphere is a step of immense significance for the sociology of knowledge. It requires the development of specialized work communities concerned with the elaboration and transmission of culture itself.

In most of the complex societies the educational system is closely integrated with the authority structure and the other specialized institutional spheres. Weber has forcefully underlined the fact that specific types of authority structures are systematically connected with certain types of educational systems; the dependence of bureaucracies on education is particularly great, as is illustrated by the case of Imperial China or the Kingdom of Prussia.

An important factor making educational systems a matter of central significance in the understanding of the distribution and control of orientations is the fact that they provide systematic and often deliberately planned channels for the transformation and placement of personnel in the social system. As such they may fulfill a multiplicity of functions, many of which are deliberately assigned to the educational system by established authority.

Among such assignments can be the general transmission of values and the inculcation of a "way of life," as in the case of the educational system of the United States in the period of heavy immigration. "Education for loyalty" of the masses is necessarily differently structured from those educational systems which provide primarily for the continuity in the style of life of specific status groups. Both "education for loyalty" and "education for an honorific style of life" (as at the top of the old British system) aim deliberately to mold the identity and loyalty of their wards as they pass through the educational channel. The differences between these systems are in the egalitarian versus the elitist emphases and the consequently different utilization of cultural values as well as of knowledge.

The other assignments of educational systems may be primarily directed to the development and transmission of specialized knowledge and skills, as they are required by the differentiated institutional spheres. Such educational tasks may be primarily intellectual-scientific, occupational, military, or religious, depending on the type of the institutional sphere with which they are linked. In every such case there is strong pressure for the independence and autonomy of the work community of educators.

The social dynamics of work communities are significant determinants of the patterns of cultural stability or change in the institutional sphere itself. Whether the educational system operates as a conservative force or as a deliberately or unwittingly used tool of innovation depends almost entirely on these dynamics in the work community of educators and on its location in the authority structure. This matter may be deferred for later discussion except for the observation that identity and loyalty focused educational systems in general tend to be more ready to "freeze" operating theories, and thus be more conservative intellectually than those focused on specilized institutional spheres. But, even this general rule must be qualified in terms of the decisive "microdynamics" affecting those directly in control of the educational organizations.

Naturally, this control is sought and indeed often gained by those groups in positions of responsible authority and power.

Education is too important a matter for the preservation and security of the state to escape the close attention of the authorities and political interest groups. However, the closeness and the directness of this control vary sharply. A specialized education may be seen as a matter of exclusive or primary concern for those specialized "interest groups" (like guilds or other trade organizations) which are directly affected. In fact, in a differentiated society all special education tends to be to some extent emancipated from the direct control of governments (but never completely so) and in the hands of "specialists." The professional educator, then, often finds himself in a most complex power situation in which he may be compelled to enter alliances with other work communities and specialized groups to protect his domain of interest from too direct an authoritative infringement. Such relatively emancipated and autonomous educational systems may develop orientations peculiar only to themselves. Since their structure and operation are largely determined by internal processes, they become themselves major sources of stability and change in the society at large.

We must return explicitly to the notion that the educational system constitutes a channel into which persons enter for "processing" so that they leave it at another time and in another social location, "transformed." * One can then distinguish between the social area of "intake," which describes all those social locations from which the young pupil may enter the channel, the criteria of selection and the standards of socialization, and the areas of "placement," that is those social locations into which the variously educated are finally "deposited." These latter are the ranges of social positions open to the student upon "graduation."

Areas of intake are always restricted, even in the most democratic and egalitarian systems known. In all empirically investigated cases of egalitarian systems there do remain certain ranges of social positions (at least at the very bottom of the social scale) from which entry into the educational system is difficult if not impossible. Moreover, differently structured components of the system, sometimes constituting clearly separate educational organizations and arrangements have their areas of intake in often sharply delimited social domains. One may think of the German *Gymnasium* around the turn of the century, when its

*For the conceptual imagery I am indebted to Professor Richard Jung.

area of intake was restrictively defined by certain elevated status categories. But social rank is not the only criterion. The limiting factors may be those of ethnicity or the traditional commitment of a group to certain institutional spheres (such as the military commitments of the Prussian *Junkers* or the Japanese *samurai*), or it may be a religious membership. In every case persons from the area of intake must have orientations that mesh with the requirements of at least the beginning phases of education and fit with the practices of "incorporating" the pupil into the educational channel. When the groups from the area of intake themselves have direct control over educational organizations and over the placement area, it is likely that they use their influence in a conservative way.

The standards of judgment for performance and selection of personnel, that is for educational testing and evaluation in the system itself often tend to differ in autonomously run systems quite sharply from those operative in almost any other domain of the society. What these standards are and how they are applied will again depend in large measure on the nature of the work group of educators and their power base. Since every such system through its selection function disburses some of society's most important rewards, the power base of those making these judgments is a significant factor in their ability to resist the various cross pressures converging on their position. In bureaucratically administered societies the work community of educators tends to relate itself to and seek its power base among the bureaucracy itself.

This process facilitates the determination of definite areas of placement for the "graduates" of educational organizations. Imperial Germany offers one example of extremely close coordination between the educational system and the bureaucracy in that the range of positions open for persons of different educational achievement, as measured by school type and years of attendance, as well as by examinations, was spelled out in minute detail. (The arrangement was known as "Berechtigungswesen.") In some other societies nothing like such an elaborate plan may be worked out without this changing the basic fact of differential placement; it has, for example, been illustrated rather dramatically for American colleges of different 'rank.'

One long range corrective in this regard is the receptivity of the placement area for the new personnel and the congruency of the orientations which they bring into their new positions with the situational requirements they find. Often educational systems are so out of phase with processes of general socio-cultural change that they prepare large numbers of persons for non-existent roles, producing potentially anomic and alienative disturbances. The potential for such disturbances cluster around all major transition points of the educational channel; it is in the placement area where they may become most acute. Corrective 'reaction' on a long range basis may become drastic.

Roles and Values

The exposition has presented at least some of the complexities involved in the distribution and control of orientations through informal and formal socialization and through the "channeling" of personnel through educational organizations. A further problem of a most general nature must be mentioned: it lies in the specification of detailed, normatively defined orientations appropriate to a particular role in relation to the usually much broader value commitments established in the processes of earlier socialization.

A person's general value commitments and frames of reference were seen to be founded on the basic anchorage of his social position in the system. Any specific role adopted by the socialized individual must also be placed into his interpretive image of society and it must be connected to his ultimate, legitimating values.

This link may be one of direct involvement, as in the case of the fanatic, or the martyr, who sees his role enactment as directly involving ultimate values. On the other hand the link may be one of a remote "derivation," where the role is defined in proximate terms, relating to immediate, "everday" concerns and the link to ultimate values is established through intermediate levels of norms and corresponding collectivities. Finally, the connection may be one of compartmentalization in which the specific role is assigned a niche to prevent the emergence of otherwise likely value conflicts.

The maintenance of the specific role orientation, once these linkages are established, is based on powerful motivational forces. They are in general those supporting the subject's "interpretive order." The balance of reward and punishment usually favors the maintenance of such roles, especially if the mechanisms of identity maintenance incorporate the role definition positively into their functional system. In addition there are established social guards against the erosion of many role orientations. They may involve control by peers, the supervision by authority figures, the reference to an explicit code, as well as the situational requirements of the encountered tasks themselves.

A clustering of such mechanisms for the maintenance and even further elaboration of a given specific role orientation is found in the epistemic communities that provide the locus for specialized reality constructs in society on the basis of work concerns or ideological commitments. Often these show tendencies toward isolation and segregation from the rest of society, and thus isolation from the generally shared reality of the interpretive order.

The orientations of the more esoteric communities of this kind must be psychologically guarded by elaborate disciplines, sometimes symbolically expressed in rituals of purification and asceticism. There are, however, myriads of cases in which ascetic practices, such as celibacy, fasting, maintaining specific postures, or others provide the psychological and possibly even the physiological support for orientations which are very far removed from the general views held by the "lay" members of the society. They are instances of especially severe segregations of the community possessing esoteric reality constructs from the realities of "everyday life." The orientational underscoring of their boundaries meshes with the corresponding situational structure; there are always corresponding mechanisms of situation control which must be involved if the specialized orientation system is to survive.

Most broad value commitments and corresponding frames of reference may be made compatible with a large range of specific role orientations. The maintenance of the broad values themselves and their change are directly determined by very broad processes of institutional functioning. There are times, however, especially those seen as "crises" in which the maintenance or the change of the values themselves comes into focus and is affected by the social organization of ideological knowledge. Some aspects of these processes will concern us again.

Consensus and Routinization

In addition to the distributional and structural phenomenon of the limitation of social and cultural horizons, differential socialization, and the links between role orientations and general

values, there is a set of specific mechanisms which inhere in
orientation systems themselves and affect the control of specific
orientations within the system. One of the most basic is the perception of consensus, which, of course, is facilitated by the fact
that the distribution of social horizons tends to separate those
holding radically different views. Perceived consensus is an important basis of reality confirmation and is linked to the system
of social sanctions which provides sometimes drastic punishments
for deviations. These are, in turn, dependent upon the mechanisms maintaining the boudaries of groups, so to speak defining
their 'internal boundaries.' There may be very serious penalties
for shifting the frame of reference, for instance for taking a play
attitude while at work.

Beyond specific sanctions there is a powerful force that retains
role specific frames of reference intact: it is the force of routinization through which orientations are fitted into a carefully controlled flow of situations. What the person deals with in the
context of his role enactments becomes after a while (if the
experiences are repetitive) so entirely familiar to him that it is
"the world as it really is." Many lose even the ability to think of
alternatives or to take known alternatives seriously because the
routine is so solidly established and embedded in perceived
consensus.

Routinization, where it occurs, is backed up not only by the
psychological comforts of familiarity but also by the whole
weight of the group or institution of which the specific role is a
part. Through routinization unproblematic models of action and
standard constructions of reality are established; they are, however, predicated to a greater or lesser degree on the assumption
that only the regularly expected situations do in fact occur. Depending on the degree of such fit between routinized orientations
and expected situations, one must distinguish between rigid and
flexible routinization.

Extreme, rigid routinization is based on a socially dangerous
assumption. It is, therefore, actually found in its most complete
form in only rare instances. Rigidly routinized orientations take
on the quality of quasi-rituals. The social structure based on it
is, to use a favored term of Leopold von Wiese's, "ossified." The
pattern can be found, for example, in those limited segments of
complex organizations that process repetitive tasks. In such instances even minor deviations from the repetitive pattern may

throw the whole organization into an uproar. The usual "bureau-cracy" jokes and anecdotes refer to this phenomenon, even though its scope in modern complex organizations is rather re-stricted. Modern organizations must deal, increasingly, with non-recurring situations. The main example of this type of routinization is found in extremely traditionalistic societies in which it is frequently linked with genuine ceremonials and rit-uals and, thus, backed up by sacred commitments. The stability of this type of routinization depends almost entirely on the reg-ularity in the flow of situations.

Flexible routinization exists where routinized patterns are established within a framework of several alternative "theories," and prearranged action models which are brought into play de-pending on "contingencies." Such routinization may be illus-trated by the most drastic examples of successful emergency oriented organizations, such as an effective field army, or a fire department in a high state of readiness. They must "pre-drill" action patterns and alternative theories corresponding to them which encompass a great variety of specific possibilities within the broad range of emergencies to which the organization must respond. The examples are extreme, but the principle holds in a large number of instances. Such alternative orientations and response patterns are available, in a limited sense, through the fact that any specific role orientation is a special case of a more general set of orientations. This specific orientation is legitimated by encompassing values, which imply broader preference sys-tems and categorical schemes than the particular role itself. Roles within an organization in general tend to be unified by the en-compassing value commitments of the organized collectivity.

In the usual run of events, the ultimate values of the collec-tivity are rarely directly, consciously applied; they do, however, remain the legitimating background of any specific role within the collectivity. Because of their generality they usually permit of several alternatives, of which the "normal" pattern of action is only one. Where the usual pattern is considered inadequate, several alternatives can be found by assessing the encompassing problem in the light of higher level values. Such value hier-archies can be demonstrated in almost every type of human group (with great variation in their range and scope); they per-form significant functions in permitting flexibility while the unity of the general frame of reference of the group remains unchallenged.

The alternatives, then, are rarely literally "pre-drilled" or even pre-established in specific detail. But the flexible routinization of group life rests on the availability of methods for the derivation of those alternative orientations which are compatible with the encompassing values. Their enactment may be seen as modifying a specific orientation while it does not endanger the stability of the basic values themselves. It is important that on certain occasions such groups underscore through ceremonial or other symbols, the lasting, sacred significance of their ultimate values. This permits the belief in the stability of encompassing orientations while permitting flexibility in the specifics; it is a special case of the stabilization of social structure.

However, there are events which throw even the most flexibly routinized role performances out of kilter; examples can be thought of among the reality shocks discussed before, in the confrontation with the entirely strange, dangerous, unforeseen, and "wrong." Such events are, of course, socially disruptive, because they can lead to entirely unforeseen consequences. They do require the adoption of new perspectives in order to assign some meaning to the strange experience. Such attempts, in turn, may be conducive to change, because they may lead persons to question the very foundation of the whole structure.

Authority and Charisma

One of the social "solutions" of problematic experiences is recourse to authority, or more precisely to "charisma." For Max Weber "charisma" was the extraordinary quality which a leader possessed in the eyes of his followers who, therefore, gave him their emotionalized obedience. We must recognize that "charisma," the quality of extraordinariness, of superiority, of mystery, is not necessarily only attributed to specific persons but that it may become a possession of institutions, of groups and organizations. This is not to deny the fact that it does tend to be personalized. Naturally, neither leaders nor institutions may, in point of fact, actually possess extraordinary qualities at all. What matters is that the believers in "charisma" have the conviction that there is somewhere direct access to a "hopeful mystery" from which the leader or the group derive superior wisdom and strength.

The appeal of charisma, thus, can successfully transcend the concretely confronted difficulties. The mysterious higher force can reconcile the irreconcilable, can make contradictions seem to disappear without recourse to logic, in short, it can create the appearance of a unitary frame of reference where in fact large inconsistencies remain. The sources of these remarkable powers of "charisma" lie in the believers' hopeful faith in the existence of a "mystery."

The mystery is phenomenologically the opposite of the feeling that the environment is entirely familiar, that it is stable, predictable and routinized. At the same time the charismatic mystery differs from the experience of the strange, unfamiliar, threatening, because it is based on a hope which overcomes anxiety. In the confrontation with something familiar, the person's orientation to his objects is fixed, routinized and unproblematic. In the reality shock of the strange, unfamiliar, at first sight "meaningless" experience, the person concedes involuntarily the inadequacy of his orientations.

Where the shock leads to the experience of the limitation of meaningfulness as such, and to the recognition of the precariousness in the person's existence, open anxiety breaks through. But in the case of charismatic commitment, hope and faith in the mystery overcome anxiety. The believer in the mystery "knows" that he is dealing with something that transcends any cognitive perspective he may have. It is a mystery not only because it is hidden, as a secret would be, but also because it is in principle incomprehensible from the frames of reference known to the believer. Mysteries always promise "revelation" in the sense that when the mystery is unearthed, it would yield new perspectives that would resolve apparent paradoxes; it then would make the riddles of life transparent.

"Mystery," then, exists in the notion that there is a reality beyond the perspective that is apparent now; it makes the faith in meaningfulness and coherence possible, when value conflicts, paradoxes, or sheer disconfirmation of expectations by the facts threaten the person with meaningless chaos. Such faith may save the individual from the brink of extreme anxiety. Faith in mystery involves an element of hope in the projection of meaning into the realm of the uncertain.

The hope may be reflected in religious convictions of salvation, or simply in the confidence in the leader's power in the face of adversity. Surely, the experience of "mystery" and the hopeful commitment to the personified leader, if it occurs, may be — as Max Weber has asserted — disruptive forces that can destroy routinized patterns and replace them with new orientations altogether. Routinization, however, as Weber also pointed out, retains the appeal to charisma in a different structurally embedded form.

Curiously enough, therefore, the charismatic appeal to mystery is frequently invoked in the defense of routinized orientations. It is a major instrument in the control of orientations in the everyday life of all societies. Ceremonials and rituals point again and again to ultimate mysteries which lie beyond even the ultimate legitimating values which are consciously expressed. Such ceremonials are often invoked by the agents of the authority system.

On the other hand, the worldly meaning of a mystery must be interpreted. This is often an assignment for experts, such as priests, philosophers or ideologists; in the hands of the alienated it can easily be used to legitimate socially innovative, revolutionary claims. The critical variable in this process is the nature of the social commitment on the part of the interpreter; we may think of Thomas Münzer, the great revolutionary and preacher of the masses, on one side, and Martin Luther, the reformer turned official theologian in the princely state, on the other. Both spoke of the same ultimate mystery, the nature of god and human salvation. But their social meanings could hardly have been more different.

The view of charisma as dependent upon faith in mystery is further strengthened by the fact that institutionalized foci of charisma, such as national shrines, high priestly offices, sacred objects are surrounded by symbols emphasizing their removal from the concerns of everday life. At times the measures taken to emphasize their sacred character border on secrecy. There are cases where the ultimate symbol of the mystery is, indeed, kept secret from all except the highly qualified few. The matter is also reflected even more forcefully in the organizational pattern of established charismatic movements. Here the "mystery" is believed to be possessed by the leader or at least accessible to him. As a consequence, his lieutenants are considered to be the initiated, partially knowing "disciples;" status or rank in such a movement frequently correlates with the degree of initiation into the leader's mystery. As a consequence, such collectivities often take on the structure of quasi-secret organizations even where the absence of external persecution makes such a pattern unnecessary and cumbersome. All these arrangements for the control and maintenance of certain orientations toward reality are of particular importance in situations of experienced conflicts.

The typical expressions of a "mystery" by its very nature cannot be in discursive symbolism. It is ceremonial and ritual. The ritual, being a nondiscursive form of symbolization, is capable of representing a vast range of possible perspectives without specifying them precisely. Ritual, then, becomes an important instrument in the control of orientations by underscoring and communicating the existence of charismatic mysteries. The ritual communicates meaning, it is true, but it does it in a vague, nonspecific sense that presents the experience of unity and continuity without committing the believer necessarily to details of specific interpretations. It further has the advantage of being capable of even extreme routinization so that the ritual itself may be entirely familiar. It thus becomes the experiential bridge between the known, unremarkable, everyday occurrences and the faith in the mysterious unification of meaning that transcends the directly given domain. It may be built into the large array of mechanisms that tend to control orientation systems in several ways: in rigid routinizations many action patterns may have direct ritual quality; or ritual may, in the case of flexible routinization, be confined to those occasions where the otherwise remote connection between proximate and ultimate values is in need of reaffirmation.

It is the authority of charisma derived from the conception of an important mystery and a hope that enables the persons to encompass within the same framework of ultimate values shifts in perspective even beyond the leeway granted him by the various levels of norms and values and by institutionalized alternatives. He can feel that everything is compatible within the structure of his interpretive order, as long as the supreme mystery encompasses it all. The sense of mystery gives role clusters a great deal of further flexibility. Yet, it is an ambivalent phenomenon, because it may be invoked in the legitimation of alienation and value changes.

Structural Alternatives

These are controls which may be operative within the domain of a collective orientation system; they are relative to institutional patterns. A final and significant mechanism of control exists in the potential availability of structured alternatives among major orientation systems within a society that capture and thus neutralize otherwise destructive stresses and strains. One may think of the interplay between Confucianism and Taoism in China which can be used as an example of such structured alternatives. Taken together, they tended to support the maintenance of the existing social arrangements.

Or else, one may think of the almost institutionalized sequential orientation systems which people in rapidly changing societies are expected to adopt. In the Twentieth Century it has become almost commonplace to expect romantic, or even radical "youth movements" to be a temporary alternative to officially sanctioned orientations; and often, indeed, the involvement is shed and the dominant orientations adopted as the individual reaches social maturity. Deviance of this kind in the orientational domain might very well be a functional element that tends to sustain a given state of affairs — as Durkheim suggested.

In spite of this formidable array of safeguards there do constantly occur changes and sometimes major breakdowns in individual and collective orientation systems. Some of them are due to the dynamics of work communities and of authority systems, others may stem from a breakdown in the control of situations so that the very unmanageability of the experience requires a change of orientations. These issues are closely intertwined and lead us to the next focus of our discussion, the regulation of situations.

Chapter VII

The Social Distribution and
Control of Situations

The social arrangements allocating and controlling situations in the context of a natural environment shape a society's situational structure. It is in the match of orientation and situation that reality constructs are born. Now the analysis must focus on the situational side of society and the distribution of things and personnel in it. The implicatons of the effects of structural arrangements for the assignment of situations and persons need to be explored and at least sketchily described.

General Determinants of Situations

Situations are settings for action, the meaning of which is subject to general cultural definition. The work situation of an accountant in a large commercial firm is allocated to him by the organizational design, the authority structure of the firm, its location in the market and in the other social relations of which it has part. These structures determine not only the nature of his formal work assignment, but specifically what he has to deal with day by day. They constrain him, they limit the scope of his realistically possible activity, as well as, more loosely, the range of things which he might conceivably believe about his situation. The situation itself involves a general assignment of tasks seen as situational "problems" awaiting solution, and of facilities such as technical instruments, and of rewards.

In general, situations are determined by the character of the natural environment, the scope and kind of social differentiation, and the availability of technologies which can be brought to bear; in short they are determined by the balance of situational constraints as against instruments of power and control at the disposal of the person and the group. In fact, the situational structure of society depends upon the quality and nature of man's power over his environment. In general, this is a matter of the kind and level of "ecological" adaptation of a society. There are obvious differences among societies not only in the scope of power, but also in the quality and nature of the instruments of

103

power available. These differences are immediately visible in the kind of situations persons in them may encounter; but they also appear in the different nature of the social mechanisms which control the allocation of situations to persons, as well as the nature of situations themselves. With a necessary simplification we can assert that these mechanisms differ with regard to the different power systems of societies.

The Structure of Power Systems and the Situational Structure

In our discussion of social interaction we found power to be a pervasive feature of interaction; its modality is dependent on the exchange processes in interaction. Societal differences in the situational structure become clear when we focus on the nature of different exchange mechanisms and the degree of their independence from the face-to-face interaction contexts.*

When social differentiation increases, self-sufficient communal and traditional economic units tend to weaken and economic dependencies are established across territorial entities and different institutional spheres. Increased social diversity within a community, as well as increased technological facilities thus pressure for the abandonment of the purely communal principle of social organization and for the separation of the institutional spheres from loyalty structures. The corresponding differentiation in the orientational structure facilitates the establishment of social commitments and boundaries which are independent of community locations. Simultaneously, the flow of situations becomes more deliberately controllable and is thus no longer basically determined by the gross fluctuations in the natural environment. The process brings about the differentiation of producers and consumers, and rulers and ruled (even though these terms do not necessarily refer to permanently separate groups in that a producer is always also a consumer, and a ruler may very well be also ruled in some other respect). The dynamics of the social structure begin to outweigh the dynamics of "nature" in the influence on situations by far.

Relations among such differentiated sectors of the society depend increasingly on more "fluid" resources of manpower and capital. The exchange element which is inherent in all interaction is given separate symbolic recognition so that it is no

---

*The discussions and analysis following in this section rest heavily on the findings and the presentation of S. N. Eisenstadt, *The Political Systems of Empires*, The Free Press of Glencoe, New York, 1963, Esp. pp. 33 ff.

longer completely embedded in the traditional interaction context. Exchange mechanisms, then, define the economic structure of societies, but their scope is not purely economic as such. In an extension of Eisenstadt's analysis we much emphasize that the modality of exchange and technology, together with the modality of political authority organization determine the nature and scope of power in the society and thus, more or less directly, the situational structure.

As power systems become independent from traditional, communal interaction contexts and are institutionalized as generalized structures, there emerge systems for the distribution of resources and rewards which are to a large extent independent of particular subgroup structures and which follow their own, inherent dynamics. Such relative separation of the major power arrangements from other aspects of the social structure is, of course, highly dependent on levels of technological development. The internal complexity of these systems makes them socially "opaque — they are not easily understood. This is the state of affairs which Karl Marx denounced as the evil product of capitalism, as the fetishism which makes man a slave to his economic productions and arrangements, so that he is no longer their master. Marx believed that the mode of production which creates commodities for market exchange lacked the transparency which older modes of production had (a sociologically somewhat questionable assertion). Simmel by contrast made the at least equally plausible argument that the depersonalization of exchange mechanisms, which reaches its highest level in the institution of money, enables men to be free in the pursuit of their own individual goals, not tightly controlled by the direct social constraints of the traditional group.*

Whatever the virtues of this debate, the historical fact of the evolution of exchange mechanisms has led to increasing complexities in the relations between situational and orientational structures, especially in those societies in which exchange is organized in terms of markets or complex organizational systems. In these cases the high level of generalization of power can sustain an otherwise unheard-of diversity of organized modes of reality construction.

One may distinguish six levels of exchange mechanisms, the

*Karl Marx, *Capital, a Critique of Political Economy*. George Simmel *Philosophie des Geldes*.

first five of which Eisenstadt describes in part following the work of Smelser.* The first type of exchange mechanisms rests in the traditional ascriptive-reciprocal interactions within a village or a group of villages, or within kinship groups. Here we are dealing with a variety of traditional arrangements for mutual help and for the distribution of goods. The scope of power and of situation control is severely limited, both in terms of time and space, and in terms of the scope of mobilizable social resources. The second type of exchange mechanisms consists of local barter arrangements, or of intermittent, not regularized trade. The third level of exchange mechanisms can be found in exchanges between different social classes, in which the right to certain services and goods is derived from ascriptive status; but it usually requires reciprocation in terms of protection and leadership. Eisenstadt mentions in this respect the various kinds of tribute brought to rulers.

The fourth kind of exchange process has been called by Smelser the "mobilizatory" type. The ruler of a political entity can mobilize the economic resources of his subjects for the implementation of his own goals. The most important instrument of this process is taxation. Rulers learn to accumulate and conserve the collective resources and turn to the regulation of trade and of prices. Trade often is of a distinctly political nature, as an instrument of foreign expansion, for the maintenance of political relations, or for the mobilization of resources for political purposes.**

The fifth level of exchange mechanisms operating can be described as that of pure market exchange. This can take the form of specialized markets for certain products, or of a self-regulating, general market exchange system. Thus far we have followed Eisenstadt's analysis; we believe it necessary to add to the foregoing a sixth level of exchange mechanisms found in the highly developed industrial-organizational social structure of today, namely the modification of both mobilizatory exchanges and markets in terms of regulations through complex organization and planning, in order to assure a certain level of situation control for the largest possible part of the population.

The interdependence between the types of exchange and the

*S. N. Eisenstadt, op. cit.

**Smelser, N. J. "A Comparative View of Exchange Systems," *Economic Development and Cultural Change*, Vol. 7, 1959, pp. 173-182.

level of technological organization is today obvious and does not need extensive documentation. The increased complexity of technological facilities requires also increased generalization of power in their social production and deployment. The complexity of technological organization in turn reinforces the complexity of exchange mechanisms.

The Allocation of Situations and Social Stratification

The social structure of power, which is the result of the state of differentiation, technology, and the nature of the exchange mechanisms and political organization operative in the society, results in a specific and often relatively stable allocation of situations to personnel. A gross description of these systems is possible in terms of the conception of social stratification, even though a full account would require a much more differentiated picture. The general image implied in the description of stratification systems as such is perfectly adequate for the illustration of the point that social mechanisms stabilize the gross allocation of situations. In this connection a stratification system is viewed merely in terms of the nature of allocations of personnel and situations. The fact that it is basically interdependent with the orientational structure and in part determined by it, follows from our earlier analyses in which the symbolic stabilization of social structures was described. It remains unchallenged, but the present focus is situational. The points are in need of illustration.

As examples, we select arbitrarily the three major systems of social stratification which could be found in European societies since the close of the Middle Ages: the status group system of old Europe, the market system of "capitalism" and the bureaucratic-organizational system of today.

The status group system consisted of differently ranked groups which held legally ascribed and defined privileges and rights. It allocated situations primarily on the basis of inherited ascriptive criteria, but exchange mechanisms are a mixture of the third and fourth levels. Its institutional basis rested on the complex of feudal-dynastic arrangements from which stemmed the conferrals of privilege or its withdrawal. The channels of personnel placement existed, it is true, in far greater number than the usual description of status "rigidity" would lead us to believe, but changes in status were generally connected with changes in legal right and, if upward, brought with them substantial benefits (as indicated by Eisenstadt's third level of exchange mechanisms concerning the relation among social "classes"). The corresponding orientational structure traditionally legitimated the existing situational structure within the religious context of Catholic Christianity. This legitimation included as an important by-product the religious derivation of power claims.

The second stratification system, that of early industrial capitalism, was described by Karl Marx. In this system power was centrally organized in terms of the market, and institutional ties tended to be increasingly replaced by the "cash nexus." Traditional privilege did not matter in the system itself; channels for the placement of personnel in this social structure depended upon the recognition and utilization of market chances. The relevant instruments of power were, thus, primarily economic and secondarily political-organizational. It is interesting to note that the corresponding orientational structure led to a frequent legitimation of power claims in terms of science, be it in the form of "scientific socialism" or "scientific social Darwinism" or other.

The third stratification system, again different, seems to be emerging in its fully developed form only in the present time. It is structured around the organizational-professional complex of highly intricate, typically intertwining organizational systems for production or control or both. The significance of the market mechanism as such and the using of market chances have dwindled under the impact of increasing organizational regulation, without disappearing. We see a mixture of "market exchange" and welfare planning. Situations are channeled to be met by "qualified" personnel, often requiring a great deal of formal education and training. The channels of placement for personnel are mostly organizationally structured and emphasize the need for a high level of social manipulative skill, educational attainment and the ability to use and arrange social and technical blueprints of organization.

Strata within these different systems of stratification vary accordingly. There are the well-known status groups of the aristocracy, the burghers, the peasantry and the like; there are the polarized classes of "capitalists" and "labor;" there are the ladder hierarchies of the organizational-professional complex that lead to a high differentiation of statuses but do not permit the easy formation of class lines. The first and undoubtedly most obvious impact of these social strata and stratification systems on the orientational structure has been described implicitly: it is the image of the social system held by persons in different social positions, images which are always connected to the model of legitimation of the authority system. The latter in turn connects it to the structure of power.

These considerations are well epitomized in the three rather simple and therefore inadequate—but still illuminating—models of the societal control of situations which social scientists have frequently used. The first of these is the type of "traditionalism." It offers the most obvious solution to the problem of the control of situations and orientations alike: routinization. The framework was typically provided by regular events over which simple, traditional societies had no control, such as the sequence of the seasons. Around the natural regularity of Spring, Summer, Fall and Winter these societies allocate to certain kinds of people typical situations and tasks within them. Traditionalism consists of a ceremonially reinforced routinization of orientations; it requires regularity in the flow of situations. Where this latter is disrupted, traditionalistic controls over orientations will tend to break down in crisis. Many examples for such events can be found in the history of traditional societies with their frequent records of chiliastic or millenarian movements which were only one possible response to such crises. This does not negate the fact that partly because of the nature of the orientational structure, the traditional systems tended to "bounce back." At any rate the completely routinized, traditional person imagined in the social scientific type construct could only cope with those situations for which he was "programmed." The lack of generalized power systems underlined the handicap.

The second such model is the type construct of market societies. Here the allocation of situations is left entirely to "market mechanisms," that is to the regularities emerging out of the uncoordinated actions of many individuals in a large collectivity. The system requires different orientations, a larger variety of working theories and corresponding frames of reference and greater flexibility.

An again different type of control over the allocation of situations is envisaged by the type construct of social planning.

Planning requires the acceptance of theories concerning the allocating mechanisms themselves and a willingness to interfere with them. In this sense social planning requires social scientific or quasi-scientific theories of society and its functioning. The conscious design of the process is to match situational demands with existing orientations or even to "produce" required orientations through education or propaganda. The scope of insight into social processes required is larger, and the control over placing people into certain situations becomes more deliberate than is the case in either of the other two type constructs. Nevertheless, the mechanisms of social planning may still lead to frequent mismatches between orientational structure and situations.

Situation Control and Interest Groups

The foregoing considerations offered some illustrations of the complex societal mechanisms operating in the allocation of situations. The correspondence between the types of stratification systems and the types of societal control mechanisms is rather obvious; it indicates the underlying factor of the social structure of power as major operative variable. Some of the more specific processes involved in the exercise of social control over situations can now be appreciated in their societal context.

These processes are most clearly observable in the behavior of "interest groups" which consciously and directly attempt to influence the general situations of those they represent. They do it often by deliberately taking the structure of exchange mechanisms, the organization of power and technology into account; however, they operate always in terms of the structured power system. Interest groups will necessarily adopt rather different strategies depending on the general social structure of power and its generalization in the society. The central question concerns the specific instruments of power to influence the allocation of situations available to them. In the group of modes of reality construction are influenced by this structure of power, both in that the "interpretive order" is affected and in that the resulting allocations of situations determine the actually confronted experiences, including work.

One may speak of an active and a passive phase in these processes in which on one hand there is the power to compel and to structure the situations for others, and on the other there is the power to accept or to refuse the allocation of situations to oneself. These are two sides of one coin, but we may conveniently look at them separately. The power to compel others may be based on control over facilities or rewards due to ownership or some other advantageous position in the exchange network; it may be based on politically backed authority and the various legitimating systems; but it may also be based on a monopoly of expert knowledge.

The power to accept or to refuse the assignment of situations requires the ability of the interest group to withhold desired goods or services, for example, to go on strike; it may be based on the refusal to consider social punishments or rewards as what they are offered, as in the case of the religious believer who does not see economic deprivation as a serious sanction; there are many such instances of mechanisms for the transvaluation of social sanctions by a group and for the build-up of a separate and distinct sanction system which offers a significant barrier to external controls.

Conflicts over contending interests often tend to be settled —if they are settled at all—through the establishment of structured normative systems which assign ranges of competence and the corresponding right to deal with a certain kind of situation (possibly only with a specified situaton) to the particular group. The most explicit such system is the "bureaucracy." Other forms of it can be found in the guild system or in labor union organizations which assure that only duly certified electricians install electrical systems, and that for the necessary masonry or other work the proper personnel is called in. Such arrangements tend to regulate and limit the operation of open market mechanisms.

Where arrangements for conflict settlements of the nature just described have been worked out, they always result in the emphasis on boundaries separating those competent to deal with the specific range of situations from others so that at least situationally specific isolation and segregation emerge. An extreme example is the cultivation of segregation in certain Indian castes which successfully attempted to remove themselves from contact with the routine flow of situations in everyday life through specialization. The effect of such boundary lines is reinforced through the resulting channeling of the flow of communications. It finds its direct expression in the specialization of reality constructs.

The situational structure, thus, limits not only the range of situations confronted by an individual, but it also restricts the instruments of power which the individual may use. Any group must be analytically seen as interest oriented and thus an "interest group" to the extent that it seeks explicit control over the social allocation of situations. This goal requires the group to operate within the structure of the stratification system in terms of the existing modalities of power. The latter are determined by the state of social differentiation, technology, the nature of the exchange mechanisms and political organization. What is meant may be illustrated by the drastically different strategies used by the "professions" in maintaining their situation control (over the clients) in different historical periods; they did elaborate for themselves rather different economic bases as well.

This encompassing nature of social power over situations makes it quite insufficient to analyze merely the "economic" base of groups and their modes of reality construction. It is, instead, necessary to unfold the whole range of strategies or instruments of power available to them and to analyze their relation to the modes of reality construction. These are, we assert, restricted by the constraints given in the nature of social situations and thus situational in our sense. The connection to reality constructs may be of three kinds: the specialization of reality constructs may flow from the fact of accomplished situation control and removal from the broad base of "everyday life;" specialized knowledge may become an instrument of power in itself; "ideologization" of knowledge may set in, in that is is used to legitimate collective identities instead of describing working realities.

Chapter VIII

The Control of Communications

The third general aspect of the social distribution and control of reality constructs lies in the channeling and control of communications. The flow of information through the network of social relations is significant whether we study the orientational or the situational structures. The discussion of this third aspect of social reality control must, therefore, straddle both our previous areas of concern.

The centrality and importance of communication confronted us before; we found that the communicative or "social" extension of reality constructs enters into the structure of symbolization itself. Building upon these general insights we now turn to selected issues which concern the modality and the flow of communication in social life. Meanings, symbolically defined, enable us to construct a stable, socially shared world, of known or at least of knowable objects. The scope of this shared world, of course, depends on the scope, the publicness, and the reliability of the communication networks with which individuals are connected. This defines the central point in our reflections on communication: it concerns the social arrangements which determine limitations and publicness in channels of communication and affect the scope of reliable access to information of whatever kind.

"Communication" includes all the "informational" aspects of the more broadly defined process of interaction. We must see the flow of communication in the interactive context as initiated by an agent who is the source of a "message" which is received by some other agent. The message may be intentionally formulated by the source-agent and directed to a particular "addressee," or it may be unwittingly "sent," or else it may be received by a person for whom it was not intended. At any rate the relation of the transmitted message to the intentionality of the source-agent raises some issues of interest: especially important are those measures which the "sender" takes to protect his message against being "overheard" by third parties or against it being "misinterpreted." These measures enter into the delimitation of a "channel" of communication, and relate to the boundaries of "epistemic communities."

The message itself has some symbolically expressed content; it is meaningful in terms of the source-agent's symbolic systems. The receiver of the message will translate it into his own terms and any given formulation of the message may in this process take on many different "layers" or shades of meaning, some of which may be entirely opposed to those intended by the initiator. For often humorous examples of this sort of thing one may look into the history of art criticism and the highly complex "explications" of the meaning allegedly inherent in a work of art.

The transmission of the message itself requires the existence of some channel of communication, some means of transferring symbols from the situation of the sorce-agent into that of the recipient. There must be some available physical means of transmission and a social relation of such a sort that it permits attentiveness and receptivity on the part of the "addressee" of the message.

The agent who receives the message or the recipient may be in fact identical with the intended recipient, or he may be a bystander who "cannot help overhearing" what is being said. He also could be what one might call a "secondary recipient" in that the originator of the message knows quite well that the other will overhear it without intending the message primarily for him. Overtones or allusions for the benefit of secondary recipients are often packed into messages. Such social relationships structure the "channel" of communication: its openness to public monitoring to various degrees, or its clear delimitation and protectedness, its location in the institutional framework, all these factors make for differences in the nature of the information flow through the channel.

If there is to be an effect of the communication, the recipients must accept it as more or less worthy of their attention. Source and channel are significant for the recipient in selecting from among the many possible items of information those to which he turns his attention. Thus, many messages are "stigmatized" as stemming from a particular source or as belonging into a particular channel. Often the communication is accompanied by messages about the nature of the communicating persons themselves and evaluated in this light.

The agent who intentionally directs a message to somebody else must identify himself as somebody deserving of attention. Moreover, he must place himself into an intelligible social context so that the "addressee" can appreciate the sender's frames of reference and their anchorage. This "placing" may be based on subtle cues; in any case they must make sure that the addressee will not only listen, but do so seriously, and that he will give the message some proper interpretation. In fact in a clearly delimited channel of communication, the frames of reference of both the source and the recipient are coordinated in specific detail. This is the case, for example, within the professional channels among scientific investigators. In addition the communicating individuals may place each other as specific persons. Complete standardization of frames of reference between sender and recipient is, however, quite possible without personal contact. Source and recipient may remain anonymous, as long as their orientations are rigorously coordinated.

The case of information flow among communicators of clearly identical frames of reference is a limiting case. More frequently, the recipient will place the initiator of the message into the context of his own image of the orientational structure of society and thus will attempt a translation of the message from the source's frame of reference into his own. The communication of experimental results among trained specialists may be used as an example of the first type of communication involving identical orientations as they are defined by the epistermology and methodology of a science. Such people are in their role "standardized observers." The other type of communication, requiring "translation" among frames of reference, is exemplified by the "placing" of some hitherto unknown political figure in the political spectrum by those who listen to his speeches. The listener will evaluate what the man has to say in terms of the relationship between his own and the speaker's orientations, he may in an extreme case simply reject the whole message as "obviously fraudulent," or he may critically examine the contents, making allowance for probable "distortions and exaggerations" on the part of the speaker, or else he may uncritically accept the whole. The outcomes depend very largely on the orientation ascribed to the speaker by the listener on the basis of his placement into the listener's image of social reality.

The message itself is likely to be accompanied by cues

intended to facilitate such placement. This imposes upon the communicator the further discipline that he must continually conform to certain patterns of communicating which are specific to the channel or to his claimed social position. Understanding the dynamics of this process allows him, within limits, to manipulate the recipient's image of his own role and position, but once he has done so, consistency is required. To use a trite example: if a chemist were to sing his experimental findings at the national convention of chemists in operatic style, their acceptance would be rather problematic. The communicator, in choosing a channel of communication, commits himself often to a particular claim of his "right" to use the channel, which may be coupled with a specific social role. This fact relates back to our basic analysis of social interaction and the stabilization of presented identities in it.

Through the choice of a symbolic mode of expression, the message itself also becomes "stigmatized" as being properly carried in the particular channel. Many communication channels require the use of very specific symbolic conventions; one may think of military or business "jargons" or the famous telegraphic style. Such conformity to the symbolic requirements of a particular channel may even give the message credibility in the absence of any knowledge about its originator or his role. The history of the arts and sciences is filled with examples for this point. Normally, however, the source is known, if not as a person, at least as a social role.

The technique for transmitting a message is, thus, always restricted by the accessible channels of communication. Their availability is an aspect of the location of a social position in the situational structure. At the same time certain modes of communication may be directly integrated with the nature of the symbolic systems used and with the social arrangements supporting a particular activity. An appropriate example is the nature of medieval disputations which was, of course, closely integrated with the nature of the philosophical systems of the time and with the social structure of the intelligentsia. Another instance is found in the rules for the reporting of experiments drawn up by the British Royal Academy that had considerable importance for the emerging structure of scientific thought. Some such channels require that their users comply with a great deal of ritual and ceremonial; only through compliance does the communicator establish himself as a legitimate user. As a consequence, this type of communication becomes highly "stylized." Certain rather specific conventions of expression are selected as appropriate; their user presents himself as "speaking the proper language" in taking the officially recognized approach to communication.

Stylization occurs with special frequency and intensity where a specifically delimited channel is accessible to the public or to some groups of secondary recipients and can be partially monitored by them. Communication between two close friends, for instance, follows often radically different courses when somebody is listening in. Stylization may be a simple device for the protection of privacy, but usually it is more than that. It restricts the range of content and modes of expressions to those generally agreed upon as proper for the channel. "Unauthorized" communications may call forth protests and interferences from the public. We will find this process of great importance in the development of special subcultures of work communities and in the maintenance of their public images.

A message, stylized or not, is always subject to interpretation by the recipient in terms of his own previously established reality constructs and frames of reference. There are few completely reliable communication networks which eliminate the distorting effects of such interpretations. They are restricted to those social domains in which frames of reference are standardized, or in which the range of diversities is known to the participants, so that reliable "translations" are possible. The social filtering and reinterpretation of messages contained in the mass media has been found to be extremely effective in making for a large diversity in the potential impact of one and the same message. Different groups tend to react differently, so that the source of mass communications, let us say a political leader, must attempt to calculate the multiplicity of effects his statement may have.

In the case of mass communications we are dealing in effect with the opposite of the clearly delimited channel. Often the sources are not easily identified (especially in the case of widely circulating rumors). Such nonstigmatized items of information are usually accorded low credibility. In other instances the source is readily identifiable, but the range of intended recipients remains entirely open. No matter whom the mass communicator had in mind, there are always secondary audiences "listening in." He thus must attempt to optimize his overall effects without diluting the message completely.

In the ordinary affairs of social life it is often vital to protect channels of communication from the unintended listener. Sometimes this is required in order to prevent overt interference; certainly it is vital to maintain control over situations. The most ubiquitous technique is that of stylization which was just mentioned. It may take the form of technical jargon; but we must also think of the many instances where messages are formulated with circumspection and care to avoid "false notes" and other deviations from the proper form.

The official standards of the channel to which the stylized message conforms may be authoritatively protected. Stylization occurs, then, where a channel is restricted to "carry" only properly screened messages as well as where the communicator must steer a cautious course among several "publics." Stylization may, in fact, border on the use of a code. The language of science is approximating the status of a generally unintelligible code which protects the channel against lay interference. A less weighty example is the "private joke." The virtuoso of communication may even be able to use several codes at once and thus keep his several audiences separate while addressing them simultaneously.

The most drastic protection of a channel is that of secrecy; in the extreme case the participants isolate themselves from all other interactions. Practices of secrecy sometimes establish very effective barriers in communications networks. They are always related to what is considered sacred, or else, strategically important information. Where secrecy is necessary, it can only exist if there are clearly defined and delimited channels of communication among those who are keeping the secret. Secrecy differs from what we may call the "distribution of ignorance"; the latter is simply the concomitant of the differentiation of limited social and cultural horizons due to restricted situational patterns. The need for secrecy accentuates the need to organize and limit channels of communication. The emphasis on stylization, on the other hand, restricts and structures what may flow through a channel and be accepted as proper, credible information about real things.

All these devices of secrecy, isolation, codes, and stylization can be found wherever a channel must be protected from the unintended or unqualified listener. This matter is of especially vital concern to those who are in the possession of a monopoly of knowledge which they intend to preserve.

There are other important matters which enter into the control of communications. Networks of communication channels within a group tend to correspond to the functioning authority arrangements in existence. The working requirements of groups and institutions create demands for certain types of operational information, leading to intensely used and finely structured communication channels. One may think of the large bureaucracy and its "chain of command" as an example of such channels; their structure, however, does not necessarily follow in every detail the structure of authority. Channels must be coordinated so that they permit the necessary information flow for ongoing operations and also allow authoritative control; specific arrangements to meet both demands can be shown in many organizations as well as in more loosely structured groups.

Communicated information easily becomes a source of power. The direct, conscious supervision of the communication network by persons in power positions occurs in all groups; the maintenance of power may at times depend on the successful manipulation of communications. In a sense, then, the user of any credible channel of communication must have an "authorization" which may be automatically assumed in the cases of those who can properly "identify themselves."

Where authority is centralized, as in a totalitarian regime, the "authorization to communicate" may be literally restricted and must be obtained by subject from case to case. Where authority is dispersed, as in the constitutional democracy, it is generally seen as vested in the status of "citizen"; its allocation is, however, always restricted. By the same token limits of greater or lesser latitude are drawn around the range of permissible topics for communication.

These facts illustrate the relationships between communication and authority systems. In general the credibility of sources of communication is enhanced, in the view of group members, by their increased prestige and authoritative standing. Authority figures of hostile out-groups tend to be devalued, of course. Within the public domain, the flow of communication is closely related to the structure of authority itself. The effects of dispersed (democratic) and centralized (authoritarian) structures were noted, as were the operative communication requirements of authoritatively regulated associations.

Specific authorities always tend to manipulate public communication, and it may be a matter of vital concern for them. This may be accomplished by the crude and primitive means of censorship and proscription or by more subtle moves of propaganda. The partial suppression of communications can be achieved, for example, by discrediting their sources or by stigmatizing certain symbols as in themselves inappropriate. The very weight of established authority usually tends to support certain channels of communication to the disadvantage of others. It is usually brought into play as the content of communication is interpreted as impinging on matters of public import; central are those concerns which touch upon the collective conception of identity and the legitimating values themselves. Even specialized channels will be subject to authoritative interference if they carry messages impinging on this area.

The impact of constituted authority is, however, always mediated by the specific social structure and the particular relations of an agent to that authority. Communication in society always must be understood as taking place within the network of social relations defined by the institutional spheres and the loyalty structures. The situational structure may deflect the flow of communications to a large extent, but the orientational structure determines their acceptance. Both are involved in the establishment of communication channels.

The overview of the social controls of communication showed a number of specific mechanisms operating to delimit channels of communication and affecting their relationships with particular contents and with the way in which the contents is symbolized. Many of these mechanisms must be conceived as devices to assure the clarity of the message or to protect the communicators against interference from third parties; but a large group, those affected by the authority structure, have the function to maintain the integration of the power system around a set of legitimating principles or values. The interplay of these controls in the context of an orientationally and situationally structured society form part of the background against which we turn to the more detailed discussion of the social organization of specialized and of ideological knowledge, which forms the content of Part III.

Part III
TWO SOCIAL FOCI OF REALITY CONSTRUCTION

Chapter IX

The Social Organization of Specialized Knowledge

In this part of our essay we turn to the discussion of the social organization of two foci of reality construction which emerged in the previous treatment as particularly important. They are the social organization of specilized working knowledge on one side, and the social organization of ideological knowledge on the other. Our decision to concentrate the analysis at these points rests on the argument that the psychological sources of "certainty" in work and in social commitments respectively find their collective organization most clearly in the epistemic communities of specialized workers on one side, and in ideologically united communities of the faithful on the other. We first take up the study of the social organization of specialized working knowledge.

Every specific mode of reality construction, and corresponding store of working knowledge constitutes a departure of some kind from the "natural reality" of everyday life. The common sense of a society always provides the broad base out of which specializations arise and to which they are connected, if sometimes only tenuously. This conception of the natural reality which common sense takes for granted arises out of the sometimes diffuse, sometimes specific reality experiences of man in his daily routines, out of the communicated and accepted reality constructs of existing special groups. In it the reality of the "thing" and of the interpretive order are partially fused so that many persons, limited by their social and cultural horizons, may be unable to distinguish precisely where one mode of reality construction leaves off and the other begins. Yet, no matter how specialized a mode of reality construction may become, no matter how "abstruse" its product may look to lay man, somewhere and sometime it must be referred back to this sphere of common sense.

We do not only mean this in the trite sense that the world renowned philosopher may have to act as a babysitter at home

or shovel the snow and thus relate to the routines customary in
his community, but we do mean it in the more significant sense
that his esoteric work (which he may be quite unable to explain
to his children or even his wife) must connect, if only by means
of lengthy social "bridges" to the reality of common sense.
What this implies will become quite clear in the course of the
argument. At this point only the misunderstanding must be
forestalled that we have left the cool detachment of sociological
analysis and joined those who cry that "knowledge must be
practical." We mean no moral admonishment but a statement of fact. All special modes of reality construction relate to
the matrix of common sense, its conception of things and its
interpretive order, albeit in complex ways. To discover the
nature of these links, the degree of remoteness and autonomy
which they permit means to discover some of the dynamics
which shape specialized knowledge, that is, a particular mode of
constructing reality.

General Conditions of Specialized Reality Construction

The most general social conditions for the possibility of
specialized reality constructs are not difficult to find. They rest
in the process of social differentiation itself and reflect the structure of the orientational and the situational order. The term
"reflect" here does not mean that there obtains "isomorphism"
between the formal structures of societies and the properties of
their symbolism—a possibility which Durkheim suggested—but
in the sense that there is a theoretical, systemic relationship
between the two.

If we are right in considering work and work roles one of the
central sources of knowledge, the degree of differentiations
among work roles, the types of generalized power and the
means of exchange must be recognized as imposing limitations
on the degree to which separate domains of reality construction
may arise as "epistemic communities" and differentiate themselves from each other. Where work is "embedded" directly into
the context of encompassing loyalties, like community and
family, without being set apart as a separate role in some
fashion, specialized orientations are unlikely to arise. The connections between the various types of experiences and the different demands made by situational problems are too direct
and tight and too integrated into the closeness of interpersonal
life for lasting, socially accepted and supported orientations

which differ from the usual "way of looking at things" to arise. Specialization of reality construction requires not merely the emergence of specialized role orientations and corresponding sets of theories, but it demands just as much the specialized channeling of the flow of situations so that they are met by those persons having an "appropriate" role. Where the allocative machinery of society is simple, where the means of exchange remain "embedded" on the context of loyalty structures; such differentiations cannot go very far. A high level in the specialization and differentiation of knowledge is unlikely in the household economies of communal settings. It requires the existence of that social distance among agents that impersonal means of exchange and highly disciplined structures of power can establish.

Even where the beginning of differentiation is established, as for example, in the peasant village of a folk society, its further development may be hampered not only by the factors mentioned, but also by the absence of means for the storage of specialized information and its transmission. Some form of writing and record keeping is essential.

The level of specialization in knowledge also is limited where work is denied at least minimal autonomy. Slave labor was in many historical periods a prime source of energy and permitted the accomplishment of large tasks, requiring sometimes gigantic efforts and armies of routine workers. It did not become in itself a social base for specialized modes of reality construction simply because of its lack of autonomy, its reliance on external direction, the minimal need and opportunity of the unfree for the development and testing of their own working theories.

As with all sociological rules of a typological nature there are "exceptions" which serve to illuminate the nature of the argument rather than distract from it. Some communal societies have developed specialized roles for experts in knowledge by providing sacred sanctions for their maintenance. The religious roles or that of the magician are obvious examples but so are those of the simple crafts. The social arrangements which supported such specialization relied on the prevalent instruments of power: sacred ones. The level of development remained limited and progressed only where further social differentiation, including political mobilization, and the development of stratification systems took place.

Our argument concerning slave labor may also be challenged. Were not Greece and Rome high civilizations whose economies rested on the work of slaves? And indeed, it is true that in these societies elaborate social differentiation built upon the base of routine work and mass effort provided by slaves. Special knowledge was possible in the "superstructure" of the citizenry. Further, there were, in fact, many levels of slaves as well as of free men, extending the range of relative work autonomy sometimes and to a limited extent even into the domain of slaves. One may remember that physicians were often slaves, yet enjoyed a privileged position.

The antique societies thus exhibited levels of differentiation not adequately understood in terms of simple images of "slavery." But they themselves illustrate the significance of our point concerning autonomy of work as a significant condition for the development of specialized reality constructs. The general trend of social change throughout world history bears out, beyond any possible doubt, that the existence of specialized modes of knowledge which depart significantly from the knowledge of the common man occurred increasingly with increased social differentiation, generalization of power and separation of the means of exchange from their communal embeddedness and progressed only where a minimum of autonomy at work was established.

"Autonomy at work" simply means that the worker must have some control over his work situation. It has many gradations, ranging from the lowest level in the case of routine work performed by a "slave" to the highest level of the recognized professional. "Autonomy at work" is a part of social freedom but not more than that. High work autonomy may be specifically defined and limited and may coexist with the relative absence of political freedom, as the situation of science in Nazi Germany illustrates.

Once autonomy is established in a differentiated work role, involving more than routine effort and requiring skill and knowledge and the making of decisions, there exists a tendency to increase it even further. This tendency is a simple and direct consequence of the attempts on the part of the worker to control his situation. It well may be one of the mainsprings of specialization in reality construction itself. The tendency, however, always exists in a field of many social forces, some of which are directly its opposite. Specialization of knowledge itself requires an internal differentiation of the work community. There must be the belief that knowledge itself is of significance; a belief often fostered by the needs of systematization for educational purposes, or by linkages to the general intellectual life.

The Knowledge Oriented Work Community

In a differentiated society in which we find sets of similar work roles, there are—sometimes clearly delimited—work based subcultures and subsocieties. In modern societies these are mostly occupational groupings; but the occupational categories in themselves are to narrow to encompass all work based differentiations of importance to us. The various monastic subcultures or the communities of literary workers, for instance, cannot be simply described as occupationally different from other groupings.

Such groups provide special orientations, regulate in large measure the flow of work situations, and maintain rather elaborate controls of communication. Thus, they become major forces in the social constructions and elaborations of reality. Where knowledge itself becomes the focus, rather than the mere tool of work, we are dealing with knowledge oriented work communities.

The word "community" has a somewhat special meaning in this context. It refers to a set of partially interlinked, basically similar work roles. Examples of such institutionalized, knowledge oriented work communities are found primarily among the professions, but other groupings, such as some crafts qualify as well. All of these examples refer to persons who face the same problems while at work, who develop in communicating with each other a more or less specialized language, and who are linked with each other and society at large through sometimes very stable institutionalized channels.

The work community, whether knowledge oriented or not, then, is a set of similar work roles which are anchored in an institutional sphere and related to a complex in the situational structure of society, that is, they deal with similar situations. The specialization and organization of work communities vary with the nature of the work focus. Examples for almost any point on the continua of knowledge specialization and of organization can be found. Specialization of knowledge is lowest in nonautonomous work efforts, where physical labor has primacy. It is highest where mastery of the work situation requires a knowledge based skill. Organization, on the other hand, may be primarily structured around the pursuit of collective interests or they may accord primacy to the skill and the mode of reality construction involved. The degree of organization can range from the highly dispersed workers who are even unaware of each other to the organized and self-consciously maintained group. In either case the work community represents a situational complex in society. The following discussion will concentrate on those work communities that have already achieved a high level in the specialization of knowledge, such as some of the specialized crafts, the sciences, the professions.

The Relations of the Work Community to its Social Setting

Major differences in the development of working theories derive from rather simple aspects of the work community's relations to its social setting. The nature of its operative focus and the relative significance of it to the functioning of the social system as a whole are among the determinants of a social location. Certain work communities, like the medical profession in the United States today, or the German university professor of the late nineteenth century, achieved a very high degree of dominance over the flow of resources, and over the recruitment to their own ranks, and high prestige. Others, such as lawyers, were by virtue of their institutional anchorage directly and powerfully integrated into the political system.

The institutional function of the work community itself, then, relates to its position of power. But it is by no means the only determinant of its social location in the power system. Alliances with or restrictions by other groups in the recruitment of personnel may be a potent factor placing the community into the system of power. One may think of the firm place which certain guilds and today some crafts unions carved for themselves in the community power systems, sometimes restricting access to membership in the community to persons of certain status or ethnic qualifications.

The overall placement of the work community is the result of the power strategies by means of which it, acting as an interest group, capitalizes on its operative work function. The temporarily stabilized general social location is expressed in the "image of the work role. Such images are always simplified and stylized representations of behavior patterns, which may correspond only loosely with the overt activities of the worker. And yet, it is the worker's role image which allows the various publics with whom the member of the work community interacts to place him into a meaningful context.

The role image must legitimize the relative autonomy over his work situation which he enjoys, and the power over others which he may exercise. The legitimation can establish a basis of trust which enables his partners to deal with him and to presume that the terms of their transactions are normatively defined. Everett C. Hughes expressed these ideas very precisely in the concepts of "license" and "mandate":— "An occupation exists in part of a successful claim of some people of license to carry out certain activities which others may not, and to do so in exchange for money, goods or services. Those who have such license will, if they have any sense of self-consciousness and solidarity, also claim a mandate to define what is proper conduct of others toward the matters concerned with their work. The license may be nothing more than permission to carry on certain narrowly technical activities, such as installing electrical equipment, which is thought dangerous to allow laymen to do. It may, however, include the right to live one's life in a style somewhat different from that of most people. The mandate may go no further than successful insistence that other people stand back and give the workers a bit of elbow room while they do their work. It may, as in the case of the modern physician, include a successful claim to supervise and determine the conditions of work of many kinds of people; in this case nurses, technicians and the many others involved in maintaining the modern medical establishment. In the extreme case it may, as in the priesthood in strongly Catholic countries, include the right to control the thoughts and beliefs of whole populations with respect to nearly all the major concerns of life." *

Both license and mandate are components of the worker's role. They are but two sides of the situation control which he must have to do his work. Their legitimation invariably relates the role to general values and facilitates the placing of its prestige.

The "role image" may be a stereotype, but it is a highly significant one. It stabilizes the often highly fluid and diverse relations which the member of the work community must have with his publics, and it organizes the reactions of members of other groups to him. He is likely at least to try to influence this image,

*Everett Cherrington Hughes, *Men and Their Work,* The Free Press of Glencoe, Ill. 1958, p. 78.

especially at those points at which it is "put to a test," or in the actual work performance before others who are not members of the work community and in the general flow of communication which forms "public opinion" and enters into the determination of "common sense." Even the most highly specialized worker must in the course of his work performance contact laymen. He may, it is true, work for and with persons whose specializations differ but slightly from his own, so that there are degrees of being a "layman." Nevertheless, at some point in the process of production or in the exercise of his skill and provision of his service, he must give knowledge and make decisions which concern persons who cannot share his specialized mode of reality construction. These points of contact are one important link between his knowledge specialization and the domain of common sense. It is at this point that a very significant evaluation of the outcome of his work takes place: it may be acceptable or unacceptable to the public.

In such areas of contact between work communities and their publics, let us say in the interaction between the owner of a television set and the repairman, an interplay of power takes place. The owner, to use a quite routine example, simply wants his set repaired and "never mind the technicalities." He applies a simple, pragmatic test to the work outcome. His interest is not in the social relationships which the repairman may have with highly specialized supply houses or with the experts who taught him his technical knowledge; he is likely to resist the intrusion of further complexity into his own situation. All the same, it is this situation and influenced by the power dynamics of it that the work of a great many others who are not present but whose performances are "embedded" in the television set itself is also being tested.

These other workers are in a sense buffered against the frustration and anger of the owner. But, of course, what happens at the "point of contact" affects them, too. The matter is much more complex where such simple pragmatic tests are not easily applied by the layman, let us say in the spheres of health, of education, of spiritual well-being. In these settings the power interactions at the points of contact will be even more important; the "tests" in such instances tend to be authoritative ones.

The successful claim to technical knowledge, like the claim of having access to a "mystery," may be potent weapons of control. As we shall see, a work community has others with which to influence the power balance at the point of contact. The control over such situations in the aggregate may be vested in an anonymous market process, or it may be subject to evaluating agencies which regulate the transactions. Many different modes of adjustment have evolved. Examples are the differences in power expressed by the relations of the "patron," the "customer," and the "client" to the worker. The patron of the traditional setting, such as the "patron of the arts" may well hold the balance of power unless it is checked by competition among patrons, ethical or esthetic standards and the like. "Patron" dominated work arrangements often tend to limit the autonomy of the worker—an example is the "patron" system which Rainer Lepsius describes for Southern Italy.*

In the case of the "customer" power operates in terms of the market dynamics. There is no specific personal power which can be exercised apart from the market situation. In the case of the "client" of the professional, it is the worker who has established sometimes almost complete situation control. In some of the professions the professional even determines to be a great extent when the work problem has been successfully solved. In such instances limited in scope as they are, the evaluation of the work performance tends to move into the internal structure of the work community and a different mode of control is established. The significant area of contract moves in these cases from the situation of actual work performance into the domain of public opinion and may be regulated by public authority. Legislative action and regulation may be a consequence.

The scope of the area of contact with the lay patron, customer, or client and its nature define some of the potential limitations of specialized knowledge. What limits to specialization the "patron" will set depends on his cultural horizons and other forces affecting him. Only in the cases of highly cultured patrons is the leeway of work autonomy likely to be wide. The relation to the customer and the market establishes a broad series of pragmatic tests. The linkage of the worker to encompassing authority systems, which is always implied in his relation to a "client,"

*M. Rainer Lepsius, "Immobilismus: das System der sozialen Stagnation in Süditalien," Jahrbüchei für Nationalokönomie und Statistik, 1965, Vol. 177, 4, pp. 304-342.

permits far remoter and technically specialized regulatory agencies.

At points of contact between specialist and layman mechanisms maintaining the specialized role orientation must be operative. His role must be protected from erosion through the temptations of bribery and exploitation. It must be emotionally "insulated" against the danger of the specialist's slipping into the orientation of his client. The establishment of social distance and the detached definition of the work problem are basic in this regard.

The maintenance of such specificity often involves the cultivated disregard for things highly valued by the outsider. In fact one may speak of a more or less systematic "transvaluation" of the values of common sense in work communities. There is a complex linkage to the work community's internal structure that reinforces these tendencies. The phenomenon of "transvaluation" can be nicely illustrated by the concealed disregard many workers hold for their customers; such has been documented for waitresses òr janitors. In fact in hotels or resorts one frequently finds a culture entirely shared by the staff which downgrades the customer. A certain balance between such derogatory feelings toward the customer (or client) with the maintenance of a "front" appears linked to the efficiency of performance. Other examples of transvaluation show the indifference of the public to certain rewards highly regarded within the community of workers. The intangibles of scientific status, the intense joy in the discovery of some minute and from the lay point of view "abstruse" phenomenon which the researcher feels, are almost incomprehensible to the lay person. The example shows the significance of transvaluations also in the knowledge oriented work community.

Equally significant for the maintenance of the specialized role in the area of contact is the fact that it is in this context that there must take place a coordination between the experiential time and space of the specialist and that of his client. There are obvious differences between the two experiential time-space systems. The specialist's "map" is structured in terms of the symbolic system of his working community, and it locates the work problem in a context which is likely to be very different from that into which it is placed by the client. What is recurring for him may be unique for the client to mention only one example of the issues involved.

We find here coordination often through explicit scheduling of activities by the specialist, where he has complete control, or through compromise schedules. Conflicts resulting from these attempted coordinations tend to reinforce the social distance between the parties.

Behind the areas of contact there may lie complex structures of resources which provide the worker with access to aid, if needed with his tools, with access to stored information, and with linkages to solidarities and rewards inaccessible to the outsider. These operative requirements enter into the determination of the internal structure of the working community.

The existence of such areas of contact in the immediate work situation and in the domain of public opinion and authority link the specialized reality constructs of the worker to the interpretive order and the conception of things prevalent in "common sense." They provide bridges, but they may be very narrow and long. The complex internal structures of working communities may make them longer yet in that they may support further specialization for which the working community itself constitutes the "lay public." The most specialized reality constructs, then, are subjected only to the most indirect linkage to the domain of common sense.

The significant point is, however, that such specialized reality constructs which may be from the prevailing common sense point of view "abstruse" or even nonsensical must be anchored in social arrangements which guarantee the support of the worker. One may think of the social setting of the medieval scholastic and his most technical and specialized knowledge. He was related to supporting groups which were not only less ignorant about his work than the public at large but also linked him to the societal distribution network for rewards and facilities. Sometimes the worker himself has to compartmentalize his role and engage in activities which "sell" in order to support his more remote specializations. Where this occurs depends entirely on the structure of the mentioned "bridges" between the working community and the domain of "common sense."

The general nature of the social support for specialized knowledge depends on the type of social organization of power and especially of exchange mechanisms prevailing in the society. In every case, naturally, the work output must be of value to somebody. It must link with the mechanisms for the allocation of rewards and facilities in the economy and the polity and in the other major institutional spheres. Specific arrangements differ correspondingly.

One may think, for example, of the differences between the situation of the professions in industrial and in medieval society. In the European Middle Age specialized knowledge was based in the priesthood or in the guilds. The universities had their origin in guilds of teachers and students sanctioned by authoritative (imperial, royal, papal or other) privilege. The nature of power in medieval society limited the scope of the market mechanisms and linked the specialist to the established hierarchies of authority. His autonomy was correspondingly restrained, it was clearly conceived and defined as a "privilege" This was quite clear in the guilds, such as those of the surgeons and pharmacists. Later in post-medieval times, we find professional specialists linked to the state bureaucracies, private industry and individual practice. The university develops into a general facility for the development, storing, and transmission of many kinds of specialized knowledge, providing a setting of uniquely central importances. Its educational and general purpose service functions enable it to establish a firm basis of support, while in turn supporting many highly diverse working communities.

The modes of remuneration vary as widely as the other aspects, from payment in kind through taxation, gifts, fees to salaries, any conceivable kind of remuneration can be exemplified. The variation in every case can be traced to the general nature of the exchange mechanism, and the power strategies of the working community itself.

Working communities always attempt to control the flow of support to it, just as they attempt to control the nature of the work situation itself. The strategies employed, of course, must operate in the given field of social power; specific arrangements may fall far short of complete situation control on the part of the working community. The recognized significance of the special work capabilities of the community has always been one very important strategic factor in this process.

What is communicated about the specialized work community to the lay public must be acceptable and considered within the range of the legitimate. This does presuppose a certain minimum of congruency among the legitimating values of the community—and the encompassing societal loyalty structure. This condition is illustrated by the case of the scientific work community.

Specialized and institutionalized science is impossible under the unreconstructed environment of tribalism or of traditionalism; it requires minimally the acceptance of disciplined rationality as values by the decisive groups. Generally important further requirements are the valuation of specialized knowledge as such.

Wherever science developed successfully, it was preceded by the establishment of a scholarly community which prepared the cultural ground for it. The requirement of value congruency in the case of science is important in at least two different respects: only where there is a sufficient cultural base for the value of science will we find it likely that young persons are broadly prepared for a scientific education and are attracted to it through the prestige of scientific pursuits, and secondly, only where such value congruency exists will we find sufficient toleration of the scientist's special role and acceptance of the privileges which he demands so that his work becomes possible.

The maintenance of value congruency in the face of increasing specialization, in the case of science as in that of many other working communities, is a precarious process. In public crises with the correspondingly increased appeal of isolative values, the range of toleration for separateness and deviation will decrease. The pursuits of the specialists then may be decried as "wild goings on," and he may become a scapegoat. Examples of direct clashes between specialized work communities and public authorities are especially well-known in the case of science, but they have also often occurred in the crafts and in technology.

The need for value congruency and a base in the domain of common sense may and often did produce attempts at accommodation which change the values of the work community. The pressure of public authority may (as in the case of the modern totalitarianisms) be insufficiently "buffered" by intervening structures and thus deflect the orientation system of the work community. An especially drastic example is furnished by certain German schools of psychology or by the instance of "Stalinist" Soviet genetics. The ability and the inclination of the work community to resist depends largely on its own power base and its internal structure. The acceptance of "authoritative tests" of theories in working communities is determined by such factors.

The final element in the required support for the work community is that in the long run it must establish itself in a niche within the general authority system of the society; its degree of autonomy is simply the amount of such authority vested in the community itself. This fact is already implied in the need for the legitimation of work activities, but more specifically, the work community must be tied into the realm of authoritative regulation; it usually attempts to influence its structure. In institutionalized communities there always emerge certain linkages to the authority "establishment," a fact which is also reflected in science through the "cooptation" of scientists and scholars into public authorities which occurs so frequently today.

In spite of the various modes in which broad social support for a specialized work community may be secured and buttressed against dangers, it does remain precarious. Not only the condition of a generally recognized failure in the work performance, a disastrous inadequacy in the output, but also conflicts with common sense, conflicts about ultimate values may become sources of disruption. Similarly, support may wane if the specialized mode of reality construction is completely absorbed into the domain of common sense so that the question arises what all the "fuss" about a claimed specialization is about. The conditions of support, thus, impose constraints and limitations on the pursuit of specialized reality constructs, but they also tend on the whole to reinforce the separateness of the frame of reference in terms of which the community observes and interprets reality. This separateness is further reinforced by the internal structure of the highly specialized community itself. Where counterforces are absent, we may even say that specialization in itself tends to produce further specialization.

The Internal Structure
Of the Highly Specialized Work Community

The internal structure of a work community tends to support the maintenance of its boundary, and by the same token, its specific frame of reference. Control over the maintenance of the frame of reference is of crucial functional importance because only through it can the standardization of observation and modes of reality construction and communication be guaranteed. The standardization of communication is often a matter of the highest operative significance to the community. This requires that the community must be able to insulate and protect itself against many social processes that have a significant impact in other areas of the social structure.

We have remarked upon the fact that a specialization is often socially located in remoteness from the areas of contact with the lay public connected to it only through lengthy links. This in itself establishes a measure of "insulation." There are, however, very significant attitudinal barriers to be considered. They add to the social insulation and protection of the community. We noted that rewards which are of high significance in the society at large are often considered of lesser significance in the community and vice versa.

We noted above that one finds communities that have reward systems which are entirely distinct from those operative outside; the monastic orders provide examples of the phenomenon. In all these cases a process of transvaluation is at work. The enforcement of community specific value systems and the corresponding allocation of rewards inside the community is influenced by it. These arrangements can be of the highest effectiveness in those cases in which the community itself has established control over the flow of its own personnel and over the allocation of situations. Members of the community in these instances are screened by agencies that control "promotion" and "demotion," even admittance to work itself, in terms of the value system and the selective criteria which it implies. The control over the advancement of priests or the appointment of university professors are examples of such internal selection mechanisms.

The selection arrangements not only enforce criteria of overt performance, but also require evaluations of attitudes and perspectives on the part of the persons in question. The separate value system, thus, is linked to the structure of rewards and is often built into a program of socialization and personnel selection. In the extreme case the community may even have complete control over its own educational system and over the flow and the assignment of personnel. In such instances there also must exist elaborate internal authority systems and jurisdictions which make for a high level of autonomous situation control on the part of the work community.

Elaborate arrangements like that require organization and internal specialization. Wherever a high level of specialization is reached, it is reflected in a multiplicity of differentiated work communities. These in turn must provide for a variety of functions; if they are primarily knowledge centered communities the processing and storing of information, education and dissemination, discover and finally, application of knowledge must be structurally provided for. Florian Znaniecki has described the role differentiation in the world of scholarship.* He distinguishes a large number of roles within scholarly work communities, such as the discoverer of truth, the systematizer, the contributor, the fighter for the truth, the eclectic and historian, the disseminator, the discoverer of facts, the discoverer of problems. All of these are functionally arranged around the cultural and organizational issues of creating and "administering" knowledge. Reality constructs must be found, stored and disseminated, the activities of persons related to them must be organized and coordinated. This gives rise to not only differentiated networks of social roles, but complex power systems.

The mode of exchange and of power relations among the members of a working community is heavily influenced by these internal arrangements. For example, where we have a high degree of authoritative coordination we are likely to find a "freezing" of the working theories on one particular level. Competition and mobility within the community tend to lead to a questioning of "established" theories and their at least potential alteration. This is one reason why science is in principle competitively, not authoritatively organized. The relations between the modes of internal organization and the frames of reference, especially the "tests" used by working communities can only be sketched at this time. Much empirical work still remains to be done.

Work communities as bounded social entities influence the identity formation of their members. In all groups the general laws of group functioning apply, of course. There must exist a distinct authority structure and leadership system that guard the collective values and regulate relations within the community and, sometimes, with its outside contacts. Consequently, the internal reward structure is closely linked with the authority system.

Because of the primary identification with a certain kind of work role, all other considerations must be subordinated to this central concern; consequently, authority in work communities

*Florian Znaniecki, *The Social Role of the Man of Knowledge*, New York, Columbia University Press, 1940.

tends to be legitimated as necessary for the proper operation of the work sphere. In fact, however, it is not difficult to discover that the establishment of an authority structure leads to the growth of "vested interests." These are conservative forces, they often interfere with the effectiveness of work itself and with the adaptability of the work community.

There is, then, a tendency to maintain an established authority structure and a system of vested interest, even where, for example, a new technology or discovery pressure for change. Coupled with the existence of vested interests inside such communities is the tendency to freeze one authoritative interpretation of that segment of the world with which the community is concerned. Actually, the work roles and their responsibilities may be reinterpreted as privileged sinecures and what was formerly a working theory may become a defensive ideology of an entrenched group.

The authorities in charge may take it upon themselves and may be pressured to do so to define an authoritative, binding interpretation of reality which has an air of finality about it. Examples can be found in the development of the crafts but also in the history of science. Scientific "schools" spring up and define vested interests and a peculiar authoritative theory. Innovation, or even more a change in theory itself, may come to be looked upon as breaches of loyalty. A challenger may then be treated as an irrelevant outsider who has no business entering the discussion at all. Worse yet, he may be the heretic who incurs the wrath and indignation of the working community.

Under such conditions we often find that the introduction of a new working theory takes on the form and requires the motivational energy of a genuine revolution, sometimes with highly political overtones. There are many examples even in the world of science where "Young Turks" overthrow the theories of the "Old Guard," and with the theories the old men themselves. The revolutions of this type may be produced by values and motives quite alien to the expected, institutionalized frame of reference. The process often proves an effective corrective for authoritative ossification of the working community. The social structure of highly adaptable and successfully innovation oriented work communities, thus, does not exclude the operation of extra-cognitive factors and "ideologization" of reality constructs, but it harnesses their energy to support the culturally defined purposes of the community.

Tests of Working Theories

The theories of a worker are tested relative to the situations to which he has access and which are defined as relevant. It is now obvious to what large extent such situations may be allocated and controlled by the working community itself. The tests of theories can be of many different varieties and are not easily systematized.

We have to fall back upon our general discussion of reality tests, and the tentative types we formed in chapter III. In the context of work, empirical-pragmatic tests are likely to predominate, sometimes with additional deductive requirements added. The working community in which the basic principle is that of the equivalence of observers, is likely to develop an authority structure and a moral system which support such tests. Only occasionally may the "mystical" test of a person claiming superior insight be honored in such communities. The authoritative tests (and their reverse, the "alienative" tests) link a theory to the interpretive order and back it (or reject it) on the grounds of the prestige of the established authority structure.

Grossly speaking and neglecting purely deductive and mystical tests, there is a polarity between the pragmatic-empirical and the authoritative reality tests which corresponds to the polarity between comprehensive and isolative values, and to the principle of equivalence and non-equivalence of observers. Both types of these tests lend themselves to institutionalization. There do occur round institutionalized patterns shifts in the quality of the tests applied; they may be from the empirical-pragmatic to the authoritative, or they may occur in the reverse direction.

The conditions under which a work community is likely to institutionalize purely pragmatic-empirical tests for its working theories require the presence of at least the following factors: acceptance, and even rewards for innovation, and a structural receptivity for new knowledge. The community itself must be organized to give primacy to work in terms of what we have called "comprehensive values." It must have the power to exclude extraneous, isolative restrictions. There must be a minimum of competitiveness among the members who are, in principle, equaly; by the same token the rewards must to some extent depend on performance in competition. The linkage of the community to the domain of common sense is likely to be technological.

The conditions for the institutionalization of purely authoritative testing and the "freezing" of theories are on the whole the opposite of those just listed. They consist in rewards for stability and attitudinal conformity and the elaboration of internally consistent idea systems. The agencies in control of the internal reward system operate on the basis of primacy given to isolative values. Social processes within the community must be regulated not so much in terms of competition, but through dominance relations and the "assignment" of worthy personnel. Where the authoritative theories are concerned with an invisible reality, it is likely that ritual or ceremonial practices are used to represent the level of reality with which the community concerns itself in order to "make it visible." Its link to the domain of common sense is likely to be regulative and ideological, not technological.

Within differentiated working communities variations around the general standards are likely to occur. They correspond to the demands of specific work situations confronted by particular subgroups and to the dynamics of authority and vested interests. Personnel concerned with the storing and the dissemination of knowledge are likely to tend in the direction of applying consistency oriented (deductive) tests, simply because their specific working reality is the symbolic system in which reality constructs are expressed, not the underlying experience. Organizers and coordinators of working communities are likely to tend in the direction of authoritative tests because of their operative focus on coordination and the relative inaccessibility of empirical test situations. The researcher and technician are likely to emphasize the empirical side, even if the general setting is an authoritative one.

As we have emphasized before: in the area of contact between the working community and the domain of common sense, a broad set of tests which combine the authoritative and pragmatic element are applied by the lay public. It operates as a basic constraint upon the permissibility of reality tests within the community.

Work Communities as Interest Groups and Relations among Communities

Every specialized working community may be considered also as an interest group that tends to gain and maintain control over its working situations, and, if it can, over adjacent areas of the social structure as well. The degree of organization, of course, varies among communities. The instruments of power available to it in a given situation will act as further modifiers of the reality constructs elaborated by the community. There is the need, for example, to manipulate its own image and to stylize the communications which reach the domain of the public. This may lead it to use its own reality constructs as an ideology, that is as a defense of its social position and an attempt to legitimate its practices, its privileges or its claims for further powers. In such struggles it may take on the qualities of an ideological movement, crusading for its ultimate values. Illustrations can be found in the history of several professions. For example, certain behavioral science theories became in the case of social work and psychology to a large extent legitimations for claims to professional competence in social reform and for the introduction of professionals into a vast variety of new settings.

Where the integration of members of a working community is accomplished into settings dominated by other working communities, as in the case of the religious adviser to a state administration or of the social scientist in medicine, they form bridges among the working communities concerned and broaden the area of contact. The very existence of such bridges may prove a restraint against the pursuit of the "pure" goals of the parent working communities. They may, in fact, militate against further specialization of the "parent" community through the forming of vested interests, or they may lead to schisms and separation.

To the degree that the division of labor in any society does form a functional system, there is interdependence among specialized communities. It may take different forms, in the sense that the output of one community becomes the basic material on which the other community performs its work, it may be contributary in some other sense, there could be shared settings and resources, as in the university. There arises frequently, a situation of conflict and competition, where incompatible claims have to be settled, such as those between chiropractors and the medical profession.

These interdependencies give rise to attempts at authoritative coordination, partly through public regulation, partly through institutionalized agreements among specific communities. Through the structures emerging in these processes, channels of communication are established which lead to the communicative coherence of working communities. One might say that to some extent there exists "free floating" information. Where, as in all industrial societies of the present, the educational system is organized as a multipurpose channel, the educational institutions become a major organizational instrument in the distribution of such information. At the highest level of cultural development, this is the domain in which the "intelligentsia" moves. Intellectuals provide many of the significant communicative bridges among working communities. Through such a position, which gives them privileged access and a wide cultural horizon, they are called upon to provide general constructs of interpretive orders and syntheses of the specialized reality constructs into coherent world views. It is the intellectual who participates on one side in highly specialized knowledge centered communities and yet bridges them, who is one of the links between the domain of specialized reality constructs and that of "ideological knowledge" to which we now turn.

Chapter X
The Social Organization of Ideological Knowledge

Work, we found, is not the only experiential basis of reality constructs. The apodictic reality which persons and groups ascribe to the contents of their beliefs, convictions, faiths, we called the reality of the interpretive order. Its experiential base lies in the emotional intensity of loyalties and commitments. A person's encompassing views of world and society, his answers to anxiously asked existential questions of life and death, create interpretations of reality which may be held with firm certainty so that the arousal of doubt, where it occurs, may signify a serious personal crisis. Such modes of reality construction are tied to the person's structured identity; he finds and defines his own being and his place in the world through these beliefs.

The Nature of "Ideology" as a Component of the Interpretive Order

The reality constructs of the interpretive order which are of an assumed or postulated "objectivity," are typically put forth with the apodictic claim that they must be true, that dissent — at least in the central spheres of belief systems — is not explainable through the mere ignorance of the dissenter, but that it may be due to his malevolence, hostility, or inherent incapacity to discover the "truth." Such beliefs are, on the whole, not likely to be subject to "editing" by work-a-day facts, a process which weeds out false guesses in the context of the empirically oriented work communities.

Religious beliefs, social or political faiths, most kinds of legitimating values rest on epistemologies and frames of reference fundamentally different from those centrally constitutive of the world of empirical work. In this domain of reality construction certainty is not usually based on the experience of mastering objects, but rather on the experience of meaningful identity in the context of social loyalties and acceptances — or on the bitter resentments of rejection and doubt.*

*Many of the concepts presented in this chapter are more fully developed in a collaborative work with Dr. John K. Rhoads; in progress.

By "ideology" we mean a limited aspect of the interpretive order of faiths and beliefs, namely, those reality constructs and values which serve to legitimate the claims for power and prestige and the activities of groups and their members. Ideologies are, thus, legitimating symbolizations; that is, they enable a group or a person to justify their activities. In so doing they also serve several other functions. It is, indeed, this functional context of social legitimation and its ramifications which defines the structure of the ideology. It becomes enmeshed and in part embedded into the dynamics of the collectivity on one side, and in the structure of individual personalities on the other. The social functions performed by ideologies cluster around the process of legitimization and the construction of collective identities which is the usual concomitant of self-justifications.

Ideologies typically assert the unity of the collectivities which they represent, or they are used as symbolic instruments for the achievement of unification. In this process they aid in the definition of collective boundaries, both external and internal. Often they limit the permissible range of specialized reality construction within specialized work communities by restricting the range of tolerated deviation. Positively, an ideology may aid in the mobilization of energies for the pursuit of collective goals and in the channeling of any hostilities against the "enemy" instead of against members of the group. Finally, we must emphasize that ideologies may serve epistemological functions by defining a collectivity's basic assumptions about the world and especially about society.

By implication, ideologies are significant within the functional contexts of personalities by legitimating their actions and claims, at least to the extent that they are encompassed by the surrounding collective system. There is even merit in the concept of "individual ideology" as a parallel to the "collective ideology" which we have been discussing. The individual, like the collectivity, tends to justify himself (as Freud says, he "rationalizes" his motivations and "projects" inacceptable motives into the objects which he confronts), and he builds up a personally acceptable image of his own identity.

The individual ideology enables the person to maintain his self esteem in the face of possible challenge from without or within. It provides him with a cognitive map of society and the world which includes his conception of personal identity, and thus aids in the reduction of emotionally intolerable uncertainty and anxiety. Hostile impulses are channeled through the individual ideology into "acceptable" directions, and the choice of action alternatives in other domains is facilitated as well.

A collective ideology, of course, can only function to the extent that it enters in functionally significant ways into the systems of self-justification and identity maintenance developed by at least some individual members of the collectivity. At the same time, the integration is never perfect, and sometimes only maintained through power and external enforcement, a situation which is, however, rather unstable. In addition, the structural focus of the collective ideology is the authority system; the organization of individual "ideologies" is structured by contrast around the conception of individual identity. The differences of these foci make for certain irreducible divergencies between the individual and the collective levels of legitimization. In no case can the analysis of collectivities avoid the assessment of the sometimes complex relations among the various collective and individual ideologies.

Our conception of ideology, thus, includes what many authors have called value systems or "master symbols".* The terminological argument is not a matter of great importance, but some remarks on it are necessary. We use the term "ideology" in spite of its shortcomings because of its familiarity and obvious appropriateness. Common usage is on our side in that social scientists generally mean by "ideology" a system of beliefs and values which legitimate collective claims.

Some may urge that the term should not apply to individual self-justifications or that in the social realm it should be restricted to self-conscious, or even only to self-consciously defensive legitimations of collective claims through abstractly elaborated beliefs. These latter phenomena are special cases of legitimating value systems, some of which are only specifically formulated in response to a challenge. We do not need to enter the argument about the advisability of a more restrictive definition of "ideology." Our preference is to apply the term to the generic phenomenon of symbolic legitimations; it is to be hoped that the various sub-categories may be kept separate as the subject matter requires it. Thus, we speak of "ideology" wherever we

*Gerth and Mills, *Character and Social Structure*, Routledge and Kegan Paul, London, 1954.

encounter explicit legitimations of claims to power and prestige and of decisions. Since these legitimations always involve reality constructions, we may also speak of "ideological knowledge."

Ideological reality constructs must thus be seen in the systemic context of group formation and maintenance just as working theories present reality constructs in the systemic contexts of work. It is not fruitful to consider ideologies simply as distortions of objective truths which are created by the loss of objectivity due to self-interested involvements. An ideology is not simply a false theory.

As a matter of fact, ideologies may very well contain reality constructs which correspond perfectly with the theories of science as the most empirically oriented type of working community. A scientific theory, like that of Darwin, may become an ideology. There is little in the inherent structure of ideologies or theories of specific work communities that allows to draw an absolute boundary between the two, merely in terms of their contents. The difference between working theories and ideologies lies, rather, in their divergent functional contexts and in the types of tests and disciplines to which they are subjected. Ideological reality constructs tend to be resistant against empirical tests as well as against the discipline of complete logical rigor.

This is the reason why Theodor Geiger can write: "Ideology is not logically, but epistemologically false. What does this error consist of? It is at least imprecise to consider ideology as a superstructure based on "real factors." It is a theoretical superstructure and, even more accurately, a re-interpretation and concealment of an emotional relation between the thinking person and the "real factors." . . . While genuine theory is oriented purely toward objects and thus "objective," "ideology" means that the thinker smuggles some component of his subjectivity into his statement. His emotional relation to the object enters as a pseudo-objective component into his statements."*

Geiger's intention in this quote is the epistemological critique of ideologies. What is important for us in this position is that the epistemological foundation of ideology is fundamentally different from that of a scientific theory or a logical or mathemati-

*Theodor Geiger, "Kritische Bemerkungen zum Begriffe der Ideologie" in *Gegenwartsprobleme der Soziologie,* Alfred Vierkandt zum 80. Geburtstag, herausgegeben von Gottfried Eisermann, Potsdam, 1949. Translation of quote by B. H.

cal theorem. Ideologies are existential complexes of meaning which are capable of rational explication only as functional components of living systems. Their cognitive structure is not necessarily coherent throughout. Specialized reality constructs we found to be components of the specialized work community; their explication requires also the reference to the situations in which they apply; this requirement was found to lead even to the "standardization" of observers and of situations in the extreme case.

The Social and Psychological Significance of Authority

Ideologies are structured on the collective level around outhorities and loyalties. Thus, ideologies contain reality constructs which in part become directly constitutive of social structure itself. Working theories are structured around and tested in working situations. We have seen that while the distinction between the two types of reality constructs is quite clear in terms of their phenomenological bases and social anchorage, many specific statements (but not all) may be incorporated both into a theoretical and an ideological context. The distinction is not always a sharp one.

In fact, we must always remind ourselves that working theories may come to play a legitimating function for the power claims of a working community. In that sense they become ideologies. In the concrete life of society there is a dynamic interplay between non-ideological, that is primarily work oriented, and ideological, that is primarily authority relevant modes of reality construction. Both modes of reality construction are products of social arrangements, of specialized work roles, including the social institutionalization of science on one hand, and of authority structures and loyalties on the other.

The argument that one and the same statement may be incorporated into both modes should not be taken to imply that it has the same meaning in both cases. The proposition of the "survival of the fittest" functions both in Darwin's biological theories and in Social Darwinism, but the context and the differing epistemologies, which specify widely divergent conditions of testing for the proposition, give it widely variant meanings in the different modes.

The sociology of knowledge necessarily encompasses both processes. It must do so, because in historical reality they interpenetrate, and often one switches into the other. Great land-marks in the construction of ideological systems always incor-porate the prevalent specialized modes of reality construction of the day and give them new meaning. We may think of such fusions in the work of Thomas Aquinas, Hegel, or Marx, a some-what arbitrary collection of authors whose work has had decisive influences in wide ranges of specialized working communities, as well as in the legitimation of authority structures.

The Organization of Authority Structures

An authority structure is the distribution of legitimate powers in a group. We are using the term "authority" in the sense of the institutionalized right to the legitimate exercise of powers. Authority is, thus, not mere power; it is not simply the ability of one person to impose his will on another, but it is legitimate power which "authorizes" certain individuals within a limited domain of social concerns to assert directivity. Authority always must legitimate itself in the face of potential challenge; there is a necessary and deep connection between authority structures and the nature and structure of ideological systems.

Even in the most centralized groups authority is rarely in the hands of only one person. In complex groups there may be dif-ferentiated and partially intersecting authority structures of many kinds, making for a highly complex system. One authority in such a system, in trying to establish its own claims, may under-mine the ideological claims of other authorities. The severalness of authority structures in complex societies itself is an inbuilt condition giving rise to at least potential ideological conflict. Within a particular, authoritatively coordinated association one is likely to find many shadings and gradations of participation in the power to issue and even to originate directives. Rarely does one find a simple polarization between those who are "in" au-thority and those who are "out." Where it does exist, however, it is a particularly potent force in the development of ideological variation and change.

The authority structure is functionally central for any col-lectivity. It organizes the group's powers for collective decision making and enables the mobilization of its collective energies in the actual pursuit of those goals decided upon. Authority figures and their symbols are so closely intertwined with the ideological symbols of group legitimation that they may come to stand for the group's identity itself and may be major forces in the establishment of group boundaries. Such authority structures are necessarily closely linked to the system for the allocation of facilities and rewards.

Authority structures are psychologically of similar centrality. Any member of any group must in some fashion come to terms with the authority structure of his group. It may assign him a specific place in a hierarchy of authorities, may give him great powers and prestige, or may exclude him from authority altogether. Some conception of the social sharing of authority, as it is implicit in the democratic concept of "citizenship," is necessary for the development of personal autonomy (even though it is not necessary that the conception take the specifically democratic, *legal* form). An authority structure is always both a system of rights and duties, but it can emphasize either one of these aspects over the other, with drastically different results.

Autonomy or heteronomy are modes of personality formation which depend directly on the outcome of the growing personality's dialogue with the existing authority structures in his social environment and on their nature. Coming to terms with the authority structure always requires the development of disciplines in the person, an internalization of his rights and duties, and thus there is likely to be ambivalence in the attitude to authority. A large variety of modes of accommodation to authority and resolutions of such ambivalence are the consequence.

Evasiveness and avoidance of authority may be one response where it is possible due to insufficient social controls. The rejection of established authorities and their claims of legitimacy is the response in those cases where the ambivalence is negatively resolved. This pattern is typically found when an individual sees himself as entirely outside the authority structure of a group significant to him. Such a situation may lead to the alienated self-understanding of those who feel themselves dominated by extraneous and hostile forces.

Where the inclusion in the authority structure is precarious, and where authority is based on heavy threats and possible punishments, holding out merely the final reward of incorporating a person into the rank of the "masters," we find the typical, intense over-commitment to the established system of the fanatic loyalist. In the cases of authority structures which permit the relatively unproblematic incorporation of individuals into their system, minimizing threats and the danger of exclusion, we find the unquestioning acceptance of the existing arrangements which, in these instances, lacks the fanatic intensity. It may also include a willingness to accept certain changes if the structure can be "connected" to the legitimating beliefs.

In any one of these circumstances the social structure of authority must be related by the individual to his own conception of identity. The central question is whether the processes of individual identity formation take the shape which permit identification with the existing authority structure or lead to an alienation from it. In either case "ideology" provides the bridge. The symbolic system of ideologies connects the functional contexts of authority in the collectivities and their legitimation on one side with the legitimation of an individual's claim to self-esteem and acceptance. Where the latter process is impossible in terms of the established collective ideology, there emerge alienative alternatives. Where it is possible, loyalty to the group and to its symbols results. The centrality of these psychological dynamics in the acceptance or rejection of ideologies helps to explain why merely economic factors in themselves do not explain either the maintenance or the challenge to authority systems, except in indirect and mediated ways.

The social organization of authority structures depends to some extent on the personal characteristics of those in leadership. But it is determined to a much larger extent by the constraints of the differentiated social system, both in the orientational and ecological senses. The acceptable modes of legitimation depend on the prevalent distribution of orientations. The instruments of power that may or must be used depend on the underlying mechanisms of the distribution of situations and the adaptive level of the society. There are, as a consequence, many different types of authority structures; Max Weber's three ideal typical presentations of traditional, legal-bureaucratic and charismatic authority highlight merely three historical especially important constellations from among the vast range of possible ones.

One might distinguish among types of authority structures in terms of the different modes of legitimations (as Weber did), or on the basis of the different instruments of power used, or on some still other bases. The most important distinction of authority structures is whether authority is seen as derived from the top of the structure, for example, "by the grace of God," or whether it is seen as derived from its bottom so that in the political domain the citizenship or the electorate is the final authority" from which all others are derived. The "citizen," of course, has legally defined rights which make him, theoretically at least, the ultimate source of recognized political authority. It is this structure which is most likely to grant the greatest leeway in the range of specialized reality constructs and of ideologies.

Authority structures are, however, not only political. They exist in all those associations which are of a more or less lasting character, whether they are embedded in the political, religious, economic or still other institutional context or in loyalty structures. These manifold authorities in differentiated societies complement and limit each other. One may think of the severe limitations imposed on intra-familial authority by the political order or of the limitations which the religious order the Middle Age imposed on the political domain.

These considerations show that a conception of authority structures which sees them merely as a "leader" or a "power elite" in juxtaposition to the mass of followers or of the "manipulated" is a simplification. Differentiated societies produce differentiated authority structures and widely divergent distributions of authority. Such levels of lower, intermediate, and finally the ultimate authorities arise in the political, as well as in other domains of social life in response to the functional requirements of coordination and communication, as well as a consequence of societal integration through "federation" of sovereign or quasi-sovereign groups.

The decentralized authorities of many different levels will necessarily lead to diversity of legitimating systems and conceptions of collective identities. It is only the highly centralized authority system which has gained a monopoly over the means of power and over the communication structure which can, in fact, impose one unified legitimating system on the whole society.

No matter how the authority structure of a society establishes its internal coherence through centralized imposition of power, through "federal" coordination, or in some other ways, there always exist distince levels of authority (which may be more or less pronounced in their separateness from each other), as well as several substantive domains in which authority functions. Each level and domain requires the existence of legitimating symbols which are utilizable by those filling positions in which decisions must be made and by those whom these decisions affect or who must carry them out. The levels of the authority structure are, thus, more or less loosely reflected in levels of ideological legitimation.

Processes of Legitimation

The importance of legitimation for the exercise of authority at any level produces necessarily a specialization of persons in the administrative staffs of authoritatively coordinated associations, as well as among the categories of persons upon whom the administrative staffs may draw for aid and advice. The roles of "leaders" in their various institutionalized, as well as charismatic forms, remain central, but they are embedded into a context of technical administrators and other experts of diverse skills. Among them there must be not only experts of decision but also experts of legitimation and communication.

Intellectuals, that is, persons whose working roles make them experts in the manipulation of symbolic systems and in communication, always have played an ambivalent but highly important role in relation to authority structures. In the first place, the intellectuals are likely to be, at least to a large extent, dependent upon specialized working communities which may not necessarily be directly linked to the dominant authority structures of the society, be they primarily political, religious, or military.

However, the social type of the intellectual does not refer primarily to the occupant of certain specialized work roles, but to the participation of persons of such working skills in symbol manipulation and in communication in the domain of "public" opinion and affairs. In differentiated societies with a market for communications and with an at least partially independent educational system, there emerges a broadly defined role of the at least in part "independent" intellectual.

The social position of intellectuals is not easily fixed with regard to the economic order or the political system. Income and power may vary very greatly. The decisive criteria of the social position are high levels of general education, the focus of the work role on some symbolic sphere, and access to and participation in the domain of public communication.

The intellectual, due to his at least in principle broader cultural and social horizons, is not specifically embedded into a particular "niche" within the structure of his society. He tends to form identifications with the encompassing communities, and in this sense, one may speak of a socially "free-floating" intelligentsia (Karl Mannheim). This term is not to be taken to imply that intellectuals are somehow miraculously exempt from social influences and determinations. It merely means that their social position tends to be related to some specialized working community while at the same time it is connected to the domain of public communications; thus, the dynamics of the intellectual's position differ, sometimes very dramatically indeed, from the processes influencing other categories of persons.

The scope of the intelligentsia depends on the degree of differentiation in the working communities and on the extent of cultural development in the different symbolic spheres. Once a social category of intellectuals has emerged, they may be tied restrictively into specific epistemic communities, as in the case of the priestly intellectual, or they may succeed in forming a communication network for the free exchange of ideas. Such a domain of communicative freedom is always socially limited, even where its scope is large indeed. But where such a sphere exists at all, it becomes one of the most important social sources of ideological stability and change in that intellectual dialogues may prepare alternative models of legitimation which, depending on rather complex social mechanisms, can at times become the enacted values of successful movements.

One of the central foci of concern for the intellectual is always the interpretive order of the society in which he lives. In large measure he may be considered an "expert in interpretation." He may become an expert of legitimation and an apologist of the existing authority relations or he may prepare the path for the withdrawal of legitimacy from the authorities. In practice it is often difficult to tell where "purely" intellectual discussion ends and where "propaganda" starts.

One major issue for the intellectual will always be the legitimacy of existing social structure and the nature of the collective identities of which the intellectual community forms a part. In this sense, at least, it is possible to understand why so many intellectuals gravitate to the seats of power and are attracted, as well as simultaneously repelled, by authority.

The intellectual community often is, precisely because of its ill-defined social position and because of its access to sometimes "deviant" sources of ideas, usually a marginal one in the surrounding society. This marginality is in part expressed in the intellectual's ambivalence concerning power; it has the import- ant implications that it aids the intellectual to see "the other side of the coin." Rarely can his commitments be simple, naive, and in that sense, wholehearted. These complexities of the in- tellectual's relations to authority have undoubtedly influenced the flowering of the widely diverse social philosophies and theories of authority.

Even where an intellectual community is relatively self-con- tained and socially based in such a way that it is protected from the pressures of the economic system and divorced from the authority structure, as was the case in Imperial Germany, the centrality of the focus on social life and its meaning remains, and the concern with legitimacy and colletive identity can be detected in even the most abstruse metaphysical systems. In these cases, however, due to the self-centeredness of the intellectual community, the belief may develop that somehow "ideas" mys- teriously determine events. This is the view which Marx and Engels criticized so incisively and justly in their "German Ideol- ogy."

Intellectuals, thus, may be practically powerless at times. Nevertheless, the development of abstract ideologies as alterna- tives to the prevailing arrangements may become matters of crucial importance if and when they become models of action and guide the mobilization of a potentially revolutionary or reforming effort.

A discussion of authority structures in complex societies must necessarily emphasize their differentiation and diversity. It is of special importance that the functions of intellectual communities in the legitimation of prevailing systems or in the development of doubt about its legitimacy and in the construction of alterna- tive images be recognized. We may even say that in the intellec- tual community there develop specialists in ideology, some of whom devote themselves entirely to the creation, the codification and further refinement of world views and values that diverge widely from existing states of affairs.

Where the intellectual community denies the prevailing sys- tem its claims to legitimacy, grave changes may be anticipated. It is a matter of great significance that the processes of identifica- tion and alienation from existing authority arrangements, which are the underlying psychological mechanisms in any ideological change, occur usually with greater rapidity and span a greater range of variation in the intellectual communities than in the population at large. The reason may be the simple fact of the larger cultural horizons which open up a greater variety of thought, or it may lie in the inherent precariousness of socially marginal intellectual positions. At any rate, the oscillations of intellectual communities may be somewhat out of phase with the identifications and alienations among the majority of the population. The origins of ideologies are very often different from the origins of the concrete action oriented social movement implementing them.

Processes of legitimation occur at the various levels of the authority structures; legitimations are always directed to the most significant audiences and must, thus, take the existing orientational structure into account. Therefore, the wider the scope of the audiences and the higher the level of the authority involved, the wider the scope of legitimation and the greater the use of vague symbolizations which permit varying interpretations as they are related to the orientational structure of the society.

orientational structure into account. Therefore, the wider the scope of legitimation and the greater the use of vague symbolizations which permit varying interpretations as they are related to the orientational structure of the society.

Such general, legitimating symbols are often abstract; but more significant is their flexibility which derives from the absence of rigorous definition. In such instances even specific, highly concrete events may become legitimating symbols since they may enter into the functional contexts of many divergent orientations, albeit in a generally "positive" way. Battles, mob scenes, the names of leaders may operate in such contexts as unifying and legitimating symbols which stand for often rather ill-defined "principles;" close investigation may reveal that they rest on the illusion of consensus, an illusion which is, however, of the greatest integrative importance. Diverse audiences can accept such symbolic legitimations while continuing to attribute divergent meanings to them. The vagueness of many supreme symbolizations tends to increase the less integrated the social structure is in other respects. Precise, conceptual legitimations, in the sense of a body of law and a constitution, can only emerge in the context of great concentrations of power in the hands of an integrated authority structure.

With decreasing levels of authority there must exist correspondingly more specific symbols of legitimation. This fact is directly reflected in the structure of ideologies as legitimating systems. Levels of authority tend to coincide, albeit very roughly, with levels in legitimating values, each of which relates to a different social context and, in the extreme instances, has a different phenomenological quality. We may distinguish between the extreme poles of ultimate and proximate values respectively. Between them there are many gradations, depending on the nature of the social structure.

Ultimate values are the most encompassing legitimating principles themselves. They are experienced directly as sources of obligation and meaning, themselves not capable of further justification except possibly through their link to a transcendent mystery. This is the level of values which the charismatic leader of Weber's classic typology represents directly. Proximate values, on the other hand, are the much more specific and "practical" legitimations of every day conduct. Often they are believed to be quite remote from the ultimate values connected to them through sometimes only tenuous links.

The content of these value levels may be referred to as belonging to the different institutional domains of the polity, the economy, of religion, the military realm and others. Depending on the relative dominance of one of these spheres, the ultimate values legitimating the whole system may be adopted from it. In the modern nation state, for example, political and economic principles are given primacy while in the medieval system religious values were prevalent.

The total legitimating system of a society, then, emerges as a complex congeries of symbolizations. Its internal coherence is not necessarily defined primarily in terms of the structure of the symbolic systems themselves. The enacted legitimations, that is, those actually referred to in the conduct of social affairs, find their coherence in the integration (or lack of it) of the society. There may be gaps or inconsistencies, due to historical facts, which determine the relative autonomy of levels of authority or domains of legitimation from each other.

Consistency of the symbolic kind is gained where intellectual experts build abstract legitimating systems in which the actual structure of social relations may only be dimly recognizable in in the logical relations among concepts. (Such abstract formulations are often, in a more restrictive terminology, called "ideologies.") The social philosophy and theology of Thomas Aquinas presents an admirable example in its internal consistency and logical rigor as against the enacted legitimating system of medievil society.

Where the abstract ideology, with its emphasis on symbolic coherence is taken as the model for the remaking of society in detail, we have what Howard Becker called the "prescriptive society" in which diversity and often individuality are restricted for the sake of the ideology. In such cases we find special instances of the attempts to implement ultimate values directly in the sphere of action; this is typically connected with the emergence of the charismatic leader, utilizing the powerful motivational forces which we discussed in the study of the control of orientations.

Ideological Change and the Range of Alternatives

Any dominant ideology, especially one maintained defensively by a group threatened by change or by hostile forces, tends to emphasize collective identities and group boundaries. It necessarily drifts into the direction of asserting isolative values. In the defense of its position repressive measures may be used and certain problem areas may be labeled as "out of bounds" and not fit for discussion. To buttress the established identity the continuity of the existing state of affairs is projected back and forward. History is appropriately rewritten.

In the integrated social system every segment must somehow come to terms with the dominant authority structure, its legitimizing ideology, and its projections of collective identity. While the concrete reactions are colorfully diverse, their major directions are limited and always relate to the existing dominant legitimating system. Variant ideologies within a society must be seen in their relation to the dominant loyalty and to the identity conceptions, including the subjective estimates of social efficacy, which the members of the society hold.*

A conviction of high social efficacy and self-confidence, coupled with a strong commitment to the existing but threatened system, may lead to the emergence of loyalistically radical movements. In such an ideology a resurrection, a revitalization of the "true" and worthy values is being attempted. Society is often believed to be in need of a purge, which will cleanse it of the destructive and pernicious elements which threaten the worthy values. Such

*The following discussion is heavily indebted to the work of Professor Rhoads.

movements are usually supported by those who see themselves incorporated into the existing authority structures, albeit marginally. It is their marginality which often explains that they tend to see a vast historical threat to existing institutions where, in fact, there exists only the personal danger of status loss. The Nazi party in Germany offered an example of these processes in their most drastic form.

In a sense the opposite of loyalistic radicalism, but in many of its external manifestations quite similar to it, is the type of ideology formation which we must call "alienative radicalism": the ideology of those who, while confident of their at least potential effectiveness, feel the existing system to be unworthy of further continuity and even to be intolerable. A frontal attack upon established institutions may be the result. Alienative radicalism substitutes a new legitimating system for the old one. Such alternative models cannot easily be taken from the past of the society since the very collective identity for which the dominant beliefs stand is in question.

Alienative radicalisms, thus, tend to construct sometimes imaginary reference groups of wider scope than the established system. It is the tendency of revolutionary forces to fight "in the name of mankind," and to adopt ideologies which give, at least verbally, wider scope to comprehensive values. The socialist movements may be thought of as examples for these processes, there is little ambiguity about their greater emphasis on comprehensive values in contrast to the isolative ones in the ideologies which they attacked. Alienative radicalisms, thus, tend to break down isolative boundaries.

An exception may be found in those instances where imperfect social integration may permit the expression of alienative impulses through the breakup of society in terms of separatist movements. Here the alienation from the established larger system may find its expression in a "loyalistic radicalism" of the smaller entity, which is the goal of the separatist movement. A curious mix of these "separatist" (and, therefore, isolative) tendencies with those of alienative radicalisms is found in the liberation movements in many former colonies; a profound conflict of values seems to be built into their very structure. Nevertheless, the generalization stands: alienative radicalisms tend to widen isolative boundaries and give wider scope to comprehensive values. This observation must be at the root of the Marxist conviction that revolutions are the "pace makers of history."

Where the perceptions of subjective efficacy do not permit the hope of changing the total system, the defense of or the estrangement from the salient values of the society may be accomplished by limiting the arena through the erection of sectarian boundaries and the concentration on personal virtue and personal hopes as the only truly important things. Accommodative sectarianisms rest on a commitment to the dominant system values in the face of a perceived threat to them, but they attempt their re-establishment in a limited social domain through personal reform and through the virtue of the believer. One may think of the Wandervogel youth movement as an example of this kind of accommodative sectarianism.

Whereas what we may call "escapist sectarianism," finally, involves the rejection of the dominant values as unworthy or irrelevant and seeks alternatives to them, the accommodative sect does not question the encompassing values themselves, but only their "distortions." Escapist sectarianism in the extreme case rejects the "world" in toto in profound alienation. Hope is seen in personal reform and in the virtue of the believer, sometimes requiring him to accept the most stringent disciplines, in order to qualify for the salvation or the rewards in store for the faithful.

These four directions of possible variant ideologies must be seen, we emphasize again, in relation to the dominant loyalties. Their contents, thus, may vary enormously. For example, the tenets of the nationalistic, loyalistic radicalisms of today's great nation states overlap in many particulars with the alienative radicalisms of the nineteenth century, that is, with the beliefs of the revolutionaries that overthrew feudal regimes and established national entities in their stead. In any case, one must speak of a dialogue among the ideologies of a society. They cannot escape the fact that they determine each other, just as the underlying stresses and strains and anxieties in the maintenance of collective identities reflect the workings of the structured social system as a whole. Therefore, we have the curious fact that many of the opposing ideologies tend to be mirror images of each other, taking polarized positions, but agreeing by implication on what the important issues really are. Still, in this historical dialogue one may see an expanding scope of social values which reflects the expanding scope of societal organizations.

Ideologies and Social Change

Ideological reality constructs have been shown to be embedded in the processes of group formation and maintenance. They are closely integrated with the authority systems which these groups evolve. They are functional components of living social systems and can only be rationally explicated in this context. Encompassing ideologies are, therefore, most powerful forces which may, indeed, at least at times limit the domains in which the free growth of specialized knowledge and the intellectual exchange of ideas are possible. It is true, in the contest of ideologies, at least in expanding societies, there is the tendency to adopt broader, more comprehensive ideological models in the long run. In this process we must recognize the interaction between the large scale dynamics that influence the formation and maintenance of collective identities in larger social systems and the in many ways different processes that occur in the working communities that elaborate specialized knowledge. Both of these components are related through the medium of the intellectuals and the societal network of communications.

Ideologies, in our sense, are necessary attributes of any group. It is impossible to believe that they, as such, will disappear, even though the degree to which abstract legitimating systems and specific symbolic models of the "proper" society find credence is a matter of historical variation. Thus, the codification of abstract ideologies may, at times, fall into disrepute. Ideological modes of reality construction, however, are integral parts of society itself and, therefore, inescapable.

Some Final Remarks

The considerations of specialized knowledge and of ideologies in their social connections and settings bring our overview of the issues in the sociology of knowledge to its conclusion. We have seen that one basic aspect of the social process is cognitive in nature and that by the same token the cognitive process is inevitably and inescapably social. The fundamental categories of object and subject were recognized as necessary social reference points in the processes of symbolic cognition. Thus, we saw social factors to be not merely effective as distorting influences upon cognition, distracting from the "objectivity" of knowledge, but we found that the very conception of objectivity requires a particular, socially defined perspective. "Objectivity" has only meaning in relation to a set of standardized observers concerning themselves with shared situations. The peculiar objectivity of science rests precisely on such social observer standardization in terms of the shared frame of reference of empirical observation.

Quite fundamentally, though, we had to emphasize the interconnections between cognitions and social structure. Social roles, as well as conceptions of individual and collective identity emerged as creative products of a constant process of interpretation. We saw every single act as participating in two contexts of potential meaning, one personal, the other collective, the latter being often organized around the arrangements of legitimate authority. The close interpenetration of social structures and ideologies became especially apparent in the last chapter.

Social roles are the major aids in the stabilization of the personal and collective aspects of orientation. In fact, we have argued that social roles provide ready, pre-established frames of reference and may even offer explanatory theories applicable to the situations allocated to the role. Such reality constructs must prove their mettle in action situations. Among these the work situations were singled out for special consideration. They require the explanation of encountered work assignments and events in the very specific sense that the worker must be able to use the explanation in the pragmatic understanding and often in the prediction of his performance and of the behavior of the objects with which he deals. Such work situations are diverse; they are embedded in the major institutional spheres of a society, but they all have in common that the worker tends to develop specialized ways of understanding, treating, and communicating that aspect of reality which is his particular domain.

There emerged from these discussions and from the analyses of the orientational, situational, and communicative aspects of social systems the special significance of two social foci for the modes of reality construction: the social setting of work and its organization into work communities and the social setting of identity constructions, of loyalties and of ideologies. Both of these major sources of reality constructs are constrained by the social context of all knowledge which were discussed in an early phase of this essay, such as the frameworks of time and space, the conception of possible value perspectives, and the structure of communications.

We have a picture of man as "knower" in his social setting. It makes clear that the meaning structure of a culture, including the reality constructs of science, require for their ultimate and rational explication an understanding of the human interdependencies and social arrangements to which they relate.